pretty little *felts*

mixed-media   *crafts*   *to tickle*   your fancy

julie collings

NORTH LIGHT BOOKS
CINCINNATI, OHIO
www.mycraftivity.com

12 11 10 09 08   5 4 3 2 1

Distributed in Canada by Fraser Direct
100 Armstrong Avenue
Georgetown, ON, Canada L7G 5S4
Tel: (905) 877-4411

Distributed in the U.K. and Europe by David & Charles
Brunel House, Newton Abbot, Devon, TQ12 4PU, England
Tel: (+44) 1626 323200, Fax: (+44) 1626 323319
E-mail: postmaster@davidandcharles.co.uk

Distributed in Australia by Capricorn Link
P.O. Box 704, S. Windsor, NSW 2756 Australia
Tel: (02) 4577-3555

Library of Congress Cataloging-in-Publication Data
Collings, Julie.
  Pretty little felts : mixed-media crafts to tickle your fancy / by Julie Collings.
    p. cm.
  Includes index.
  ISBN-13: 978-1-60061-090-5 (alk. paper)
  1. Felt work. I. Title.
  TT849.5.C62 2008
  746'.0463--dc22
                    2008010085

 www.fwpublications.com

F+W PUBLICATIONS, INC.

editor: JESSICA GORDON
designer: JENNIFER HOFFMAN
production coordinator: GREG NOCK
photo stylist: JAN NICKUM
photographers: CHRISTINE POLOMSKY, TIM GRONDIN & JOHN CARRICO, ADAM LEIGH-MANUELL, ADAM HENRY, ALIAS IMAGING, LLC

METRIC CONVERSION CHART

to convert	to	multiply by
inches	centimeters	2.54
centimeters	inches	0.4
feet	centimeters	30.5
centimeters	feet	0.03
yards	meters	0.9
meters	yards	1.1
sq. inches	sq. centimeters	6.45
sq. centimeters	sq. inches	0.16
sq. feet	sq. meters	0.09
sq. meters	sq. feet	10.8
sq. yards	sq. meters	0.8
sq. meters	sq. yards	1.2
pounds	kilograms	0.45
kilograms	pounds	2.2
ounces	grams	28.3
grams	ounces	0.035

acknowledgments

Thank you to the many wonderful people who guided me along my way while I was working on this book:

To my editor, Jessica Gordon, for being able to put so beautifully on paper all my dreams of wool felt and for letting me cut up her pink skirt.

To Christine Polomsky for her amazing photographs and for making me feel so at home in her studio.

To everyone at North Light who showed such genuine support for my book, thank you all for your creative voices.

Thank you to my family for the many times you worked together to help me meet a deadline and write this book.

Matt, thank you for making me laugh every day.

Marina, thank you for sharing your creative energy.

Hannah, thank you for being such an amazing shopper.

Burke, thank you for letting me take over the computer.

Olivia, thank you for letting your favorite things be sent away to be photographed for this book.

i Adore yOu alL.

dedication

This book is dedicated to my mother, Joan, and my grandmother Eloise, who always made beautiful things with their hands.

introduction

FROM THE TIME WE WERE LITTLE GIRLS, MY FOUR CREATIVE SISTERS AND I WERE ALWAYS MAKING THINGS. We sewed and painted, glued and baked, and cut and colored. Our endless creative messes were the beginning of my adventures in crafting, which have continued into adulthood. Over the years, I have learned to knit, dye and even spin my own yarns. I love working with wool so much I nearly bought a sheep, but my husband said our neighbors would object.

As a compromise to owning an actual sheep, I began gathering bits of wool left over from sewing projects and taking apart old wool clothing to use in my designs. I love working with wool felt—it dyes beautifully, cuts and sews without fraying, and adds a soft organic feel to all my projects.

Throughout this book you'll find unusual materials, such as metal screen from the hardware store and a vintage cardboard sewing kit, combined with wool felt (see the *Quiet Book*, page 58, and the *Needle Book*, page 52, respectively). Paper, metal, beads and glass are also mixed with wool to create lovely dimensionality and touchable textures in jewelry pieces such as the *Felt Charm Bracelet* (see page 76). You'll also find projects calling for unexpected elements, like a discarded book or a single vintage earring. Each found item adds a special touch. Look through your collection of quirky treasures and prized vintage finds and use them to create your own *Pretty Little Felts*.

materials

The basic materials for making the projects in this book are felt, fabric, paper and glue. Pretty ribbons, beads, trims and threads add a lovely decorative touch to your pieces, while a bit of glass glitter and mica adds a gorgeous sparkle. I have used some vintage items from my collection that you can substitute with anything you like. Look through the things you have been drawn to and find a new way to use the treasures you have gathered. The resource list beginning on page 124 will help you locate any additional materials you may need.

WOOL FELT is becoming readily available and can be purchased by the square or by the yard. You may also find some great pieces of wool by deconstructing old clothing. You can felt wool to make a denser fabric, or leave it unfelted if it's woven tightly enough that it won't unravel when cut.

WOOL ROVING is a term used to describe wool fibers that have been washed and combed into a loose roll. Roving may be purchased dyed or undyed in bundles, hanks or by the foot.

PATTERNED COTTON FABRICS can be found at quilting or craft stores. Some vintage cotton pieces cut from old aprons or clothing have wonderful colors and retro designs and are a fun addition to your projects.

RIBBONS & TRIMS can be gathered from old sewing baskets, cut from worn doll clothes or purchased at a fabric store. Vintage ribbons and trims that have been stained and wrinkled can be lovely additions just as they are.

STRINGS used for crocheting and tatting can be found wound into balls around small pieces of cardboard tubing. The lovely threads can be used for embroidery and for tying on decorative elements. Wrap your strings around old wooden thread spools for easy use.

NEEDLES of several different sizes will be useful when making the projects in this book. Locate small, sharp hand-sewing needles for sewing thread, assorted embroidery needles in sizes 5 to 10 to accommodate one to six strands of floss, and a large-eyed sharp needle that will work with elastic stretch cord.

Opposite page, clockwise from top left: glitter, strings, vintage beads, vintage music pages, dyed wool felt, vintage clip-on earrings and buttons, ribbon, vintage lace trim.

EMBROIDERY FLOSS is sold in small hanks of multi-stranded threads and can be separated for sewing fine details or used with several strands together for more defined stitches. Wool embroidery threads add a beautiful texture.

SEWING THREADS can be used with your sewing machine or for hand-stitching. Vintage spools of silk and mercerized cotton add a lovely sheen when stitched on wool felt.

SILK & VELVET FLOWERS from your craft store can be pulled off their plastic stems and sewn or glued onto your projects. Some of my favorites are old millinery flowers and pieces I have carefully removed from vintage ladies' hats.

BEADS in all shapes and sizes can be purchased singly or in packets. Seed beads are small glass beads, sometimes lined in silver for extra sparkle, that can be sewn onto any kind of wool. Many old broken jewelry pieces can be carefully deconstructed so the beads can be used in new designs.

BUTTONS can be made from mother of pearl, plastic, metal, glass, rhinestones, enamel and carved bone. Look for unusual and decorative buttons to use in your projects.

GLASS GLITTER is actually made from shards of sparkling glass. It comes in many colors and can be purchased in an extra-fine to coarse grain. Take care when handling the glitter, as it is very sharp.

MICA is a shimmery mineral that can be processed into small flakes that add a beautiful vintage sparkle.

ACRYLIC PAINT & GESSO are used throughout the book to add color and texture. Fluid acrylics produce a more transparent wash of color while acrylic craft paint is thicker and more opaque.

PAINTBRUSHES in several sizes are very useful. A fine detail brush, a medium round brush and a large flat brush for acrylics are the three basic brushes to have on hand.

PAGES from old books, dictionaries, musical scores and magazines provide a varied collection of text and images.

TACKY GLUE is an all-purpose, versatile white glue that dries clear and works well with paper and fabric.

ACRYLIC GEL MEDIUM is transparent and works well as a final surface coat or sealer and also as a base coat for attaching dimensional items. Gel medium comes in either a gloss or matte finish.

A collection of basic tools used for crafting will be all you need to complete most projects in this book. A sewing machine is used for a couple of projects, but you can easily substitute hand-sewing if desired.

SCISSORS for fabric and paper are used throughout the book. I mark my fabric scissors to remind my family to use them only on fabric. My favorite paper scissors are the small, sharp-pointed Fiskars.

PINKING SHEARS & SCALLOP-EDGE SHEARS for fabric cut a nice edge on wool felt. Many small decorative-edge scissors will work only on paper, so try them first before you buy them to use on felt.

METAL SNIPS are helpful for cutting metal and wire. I purchased them to cut up old tin containers, and they work very well.

A CRAFT KNIFE is perfect for cutting out fine detailed shapes in paper and cardboard. Replace your blade regularly so the knife cuts cleanly without tearing. Use a self-healing mat with your craft knife to protect your work surface, and use a metal-edge ruler for making straight cuts.

A ROTARY CUTTER makes smooth, even cuts through even thick wool felt. This tool is especially useful for cutting thin strips.

A CLEAR PLASTIC GRIDDED RULER with one metal edge and one beveled edge is indispensable for cutting and marking paper and fabric. The grid is helpful for measuring and marking evenly.

AN EYELET SETTER is used for setting eyelets by pressing the metal shaft into an even flange over paper or felt. Set the eyelet using a small hammer and a self-healing mat to protect your work surface.

A HOLE PUNCH is useful for making perfect holes in paper. It's a good idea to collect a few punches in the most basic sizes, including $\frac{1}{16}$" (2mm), $\frac{1}{8}$" (3mm), and $\frac{1}{4}$" (6mm). A Japanese screw hole punch is wonderful for punching heavy cardboard, wool felt and fabric.

A NEEDLE-FELTING NEEDLE is a long, barbed needle used to felt together wool fibers while working over a needle-felting base. A single medium-sized needle will work well for the projects in this book.

A CIRCLE TEMPLATE is used to mark circles and measure felt balls. Select one that has a variety of sizes. Staedtler Mars makes a template for circles $\frac{1}{16}$" (2mm) to $1\frac{7}{8}$" (5cm) circles.

WIRE CUTTERS are used for cutting thin-gauge wire. A small pair of nail clippers set aside for clipping wire is a handy tool, but for making jewelry a nice set of flush cutters will give your wire ends a professional finish.

FLAT-NOSE PLIERS have a flat edge at the tip of the jaw for wrapping wire. Also use them for bending wire and opening and closing jump rings.

ROUND-NOSE PLIERS have rounded, cone-shaped tapering pincers for making small loops and bends in wire.

Opposite page, from left to right, top to bottom: selection of decorative-edge scissors, buttons, thimble, pins and needles in pincushion, flush cutters, round-nose pliers, felt squares, small and large scissors, rotary cutter, ruler, craft knife, eyelet setter, snips, flat-nose pliers.

techniques

If you have never worked with wool or wool felt, you will enjoy discovering how wonderful it feels to work with. Wool has interesting textures and depth, it cuts beautifully and the needle floats through the fabric as you are sewing. Four basic techniques are described in this section to get you started.

DECONSTRUCTING takes you through the basics of recycling old clothing and blankets for unusual and high-quality wool pieces. The DYEING section offers suggestions for using simple permanent dyes to alter the look of small wool pieces. WET FELTING is the beginner's guide to felting wool fibers into beads and balls. FIVE BASIC STITCHES are illustrated in the stitching section for decorating your projects with colorful threads.

TO FELT OR NOT TO FELT

If you are deciding whether or not to felt a piece of wool fabric, keep a few things in mind:

Examine the cut edge. Is the fabric thin or loosely woven? Are there loose threads around the edges? If the wool felt is solid and tightly woven, you do not need to felt it. Otherwise, it's best to felt the wool. The felting process shrinks the fabric by interlocking the wool fibers, creating a denser fabric that will not fray along the edges.

To felt your piece of wool fabric, toss it in the washing machine with warm water and some detergent. Allow your washer to go through a full cycle. Remove the wool and check to see how much the fabric has shrunk. If you like the feel of the wool, spread it out on a flat surface and let it air dry. If the fabric still feels a bit thin or loose, put the wool fabric in the dryer on a cotton setting with an old towel and allow it to dry.

Remember: Only felt wool pieces of the same color in the washer, because the colored wool fibers will transfer from one piece to another.

Deconstructing

Vintage wool clothing and blankets are great sources of wool for dyeing, felting and using in your projects. Look through secondhand stores and vintage shops for old clothing made with 100-percent wool. I like to find unusual colors and weaves that will overdye well, and I also look for examples of fine smooth wool of a high grade. Keep in mind the wool from most overcoats will be a heavier weight and may not need additional felting. When taking apart clothing, You can keep just the bigger pieces and discard the small leftovers such as plackets, cuffs and collars, as well as pieces with buttonholes that would be time consuming to unpick. Or you can plan to use these unusual elements as part of your design. Don't worry about stains or moth holes, as you can cut around these, or intentionally use them in your design. Look carefully before buying clothing made for children and dolls to be sure the pieces will be large enough to use after cutting apart. Wash everything even if you are not planning to felt the wool further. I like to save the old buttons and garment labels from vintage clothing to use in other projects.

Deconstructing a Jacket

To deconstruct a jacket, cut along the seams to remove the sleeves, lining, pockets and collar. A seam ripper can be used to take out the hems. Wash the wool pieces in the washing machine in warm water with detergent, and air dry them if you like the feel of the wool, or machine dry them if you want to felt the fabric a bit more.

Deconstructing a Skirt

A beautiful old wool skirt is very easy to take apart to use in your wool felt projects. Skirts have few seams and yield large pieces of felt. Most often the wool used to make skirts is of a medium weight and may be a fun plaid or herringbone weave.

{1} DECIDE WHERE TO CUT: Lay your skirt out on a table or flat work surface and examine it to see where the seams are.

{2} CUT ALONG SIDE SEAM: Separate the skirt from the lining if there is one and begin cutting at the side seam. Cut around any pockets, following the seam to the waistband. Repeat for the other side seam.

{3} CUT OFF WAISTBAND: Cut the skirt front away from the waistband as shown.

{4} CLEAN AND FELT WOOL PIECES: Discard the waistband, zipper and lining unless you plan to use them in another project. Wash the wool pieces from each item together, separating them from other wool pieces so the different colored fibers don't get felted to each other. Air dry the wool pieces flat or machine dry them to further felt the fibers. Press the fabrics with an iron set on the wool setting, using steam to press the pieces flat. Now you are ready to dream up ways to use your felt.

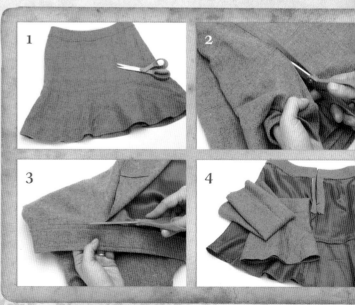

Dyeing

Dyeing wool is always an experiment because the colors react so differently with each piece of wool, but I think you'll find that you're very pleased and sometimes quite surprised with the results. Dyeing your wool pieces can give you a broader range of colors to work with. One hundred percent wool is better than a wool-blend fabric for dyeing as it will take the color more evenly. However, some wool blends will dye well—just test a small piece of a wool blend in a dye bath before dyeing a large amount to see how the fabric will accept the dye.

There are many different kinds of dye you can experiment with to dye your wool. Look for permanent dyes that won't bleed out of your fabric over time or with washing.

Dyes that come in a liquid form are easy to add to water, and they mix well. Powdered dyes can be messy to use, but I like them as I can control the concentration of color better. See the resource list of dye manufacturers on page 125.

Eight different wool swatches were dipped in blue, red and green dye to show how overdyeing (applying dye to an already-dyed fabric) changes the color of the wool. The top row of swatches shows the felt pieces before dyeing for reference. You will notice some pieces changed color only a little, while the pale yellow swatch was altered dramatically by the dyes.

Pickle Jar Dip Dyeing

I first started using leftover pickle jars for dyeing small batches of wool yarn. I liked that the lid fit on tight and I could make color changes on a small scale. The jars are a great size for dyeing small pieces of wool. Collect several jars in varying sizes so when you begin dyeing your wool pieces you can dye several batches at a time. Permanent dyes will stain fabrics and skin, so wear a protective apron and gloves if desired.

{1} MIX DYE. Fill a small pickle jar or any other glass jar half full with clean, warm water. Add a few drops of liquid dye, or any other dye you like. Stir the liquid gently to thoroughly mix the dye.

{2} SUBMERGE FELT IN WATER. Submerge all of the felt pieces to be dyed in clean, warm water. If you want the felt to dye evenly, it needs to be uniformly wet. If you want to try different effects, you can leave some of the felt dry.

{3} DYE FELT. Mix up any other dyes you like, using any kind of dyeing solution, including powder or liquid forms of dye. Submerge small pieces of dampened felt in each dye jar and secure the lid. Leave the felt in the dye for a longer time if you want the color to be more saturated. Leave it for just a few minutes if you want a lighter color. The fiber content determines how well the fabric accepts the dye.

{4} REMOVE FELT FROM DYE. Use tweezers to remove each dyed piece of felt from its pickle jar.

{5} RINSE DYED PIECES. Submerge the dyed pieces in clean, cool water and rinse them until the water runs clear.

{6} DRY DYED PIECES AND IRON. Lay the dyed pieces out to dry on a clean towel. Pat them a bit to squeeze out excess water and to begin the drying process. The color will lighten as the fabric dries. When the pieces are dry, iron them on the wool setting to help heat-set the color.

Wet Felting Beads

Wool roving can be used to make beautiful wool beads of any size and shape. The process is very simple. Start with wool dyed or undyed roving, and roll it into a loose ball. Fill a basin with quite warm water and a little soap to help the wool fibers open, and submerge the wool. Create friction by rolling the ball between your hands, forcing the fibers to interconnect and felt together. Stop rolling the ball at the soft-bead stage if you are making Flower Bun Beads (see page 91), or continue felting your ball to the hard-bead stage if you will be cutting the bead in half for a project like the *Flower Ball Rings* (see page 88).

At the soft-bead stage, the bead is round and defined, but only semi-firm if you squish it. This loft allows for the bead to puff out around the stitching. At the hard-bead stage, the bead is tightly felted, round and very dense. It feels very firm and compact when you squish it. The hard bead holds its shape well when cut in half.

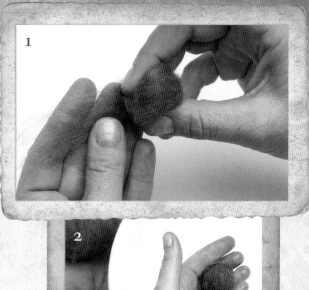

{1} SHAPE ROVING INTO BALL: Pull out a bit of wool roving. Wind the wool up into a ball shape, keeping the fine wool fibers at the end wrapped around the ball. Your ball will shrink about in half as it felts, so start with a bigger ball than the size of bead you want. Experiment a bit to get the finished size you want.

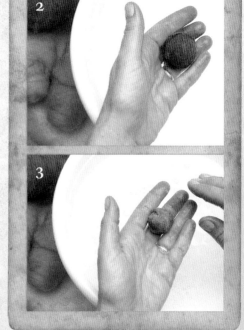

{2} SUBMERGE BALL IN WARM, SOAPY WATER: Dip the wool in very warm water with a bit of dish soap added.

{3} GENTLY ROLL BALL TO BEGIN FELTING: Add a tiny drop of soap to your hands and begin gently rolling the wool ball as if you were rolling a ball of clay. Dip the felt back in the warm water every 3 or 4 rolls. Continue rolling until the ball starts to condense a bit.

{4} ADD SOAP AND CONTINUE FELTING: Add a few more drops of soap to your hands. Begin adding a bit more pressure as you roll your ball, and continue to dip it in the sudsy water every so often. Gentle pressure in the beginning helps your bead to be round and smooth without any folds over the surface.

{5} DETERMINE IF BALL IS CORRECT SIZE: Rinse your bead in clear water and blot it dry by rolling it on a towel. Check the size of your ball with a circle template. Then shape the bead and air dry it overnight.

Wool roving can be purchased already dyed in a gorgeous palette of colors.
It's available in convenient bundles, wound into skeins or sold by the foot.

Stitching

Wool felt is wonderful to stitch and sew because the edges do not fray and the fabric is soft and pliable. A few basic embroidery stitches will add fun and flair to your felt projects. I use six-strand embroidery floss for most projects, separating the strands to use one or two at a time for a fine stitch or using all six strands together for a thicker, more defined stitch. Embroidery needles have large eyes and come in several sizes. An assorted pack of size 5 through 10 needles will offer a range of needle sizes for stitching on felt.

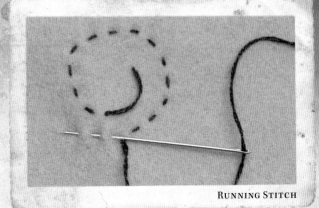

RUNNING STITCH

Running Stitch

The running stitch is a basic stitch used to sew two fabrics together and to create a line. Work in running stitch by poking the needle in and out of the fabric at regular intervals.

Backstitch

The backstitch can be used to stitch a curved or a straight line. Poke the needle up through the fabric where the first stitch will end. Pull the thread through. Poke the needle down through the fabric to the right to complete the first stitch, then up through the fabric to the left an even distance away. Continue along the stitching line.

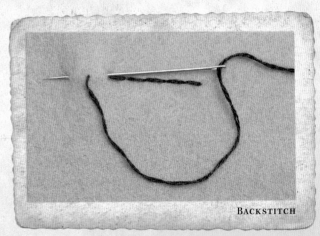

BACKSTITCH

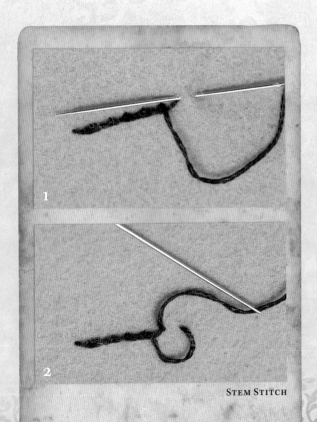

STEM STITCH

Stem Stitch

{1} BRING NEEDLE DOWN AND UP AT BASE OF LAST STITCH: The stem stitch can be used to outline and to make flower stems. Working from left to right, start by poking the needle up through the fabric where your first stitch will start. Poke the needle down through the fabric to the right where the stitch will end and back up in the middle of the stitch as shown. Pull the thread snug. Poke your needle down through your fabric to the right so half of your second stitch overlaps the first stitch and extends to the right an equal distance away.

{2} PULL STITCH TIGHT: Continue to sew even stitches along the stitching line, each time bringing the needle up while holding the thread down below the needle.

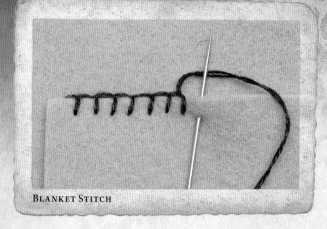

BLANKET STITCH

Blanket Stitch

This stitch will bind off a raw edge or attach another felt shape to a base fabric. The stitch is worked left to right. Begin with the thread at the edge of the fabric or shape. Poke the needle down through the fabric ¼" (6mm) in from the edge and ¼" (6mm) to the right of the thread, then up at the edge straight up from your needle. Keep the needle over the thread as shown while pulling the thread snug.

Daisy Stitch

{1} CREATE PETAL SHAPE: Poke your needle up through the fabric at the base of the petal. Poke the needle down through the fabric next to the thread at the base of the petal, then pull the thread to close the loop to the correct size. Poke your needle up through the fabric at the end of the petal where the stitch will secure the thread.

{2} SECURE PETAL SHAPE: Poke the needle down through the fabric on the other side of the looped thread and pull it snug. Poke the needle up at the base of the next petal.

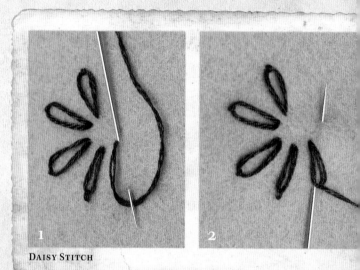

DAISY STITCH

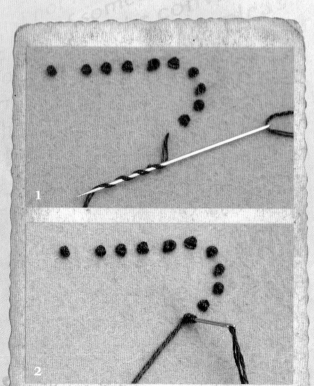

FRENCH KNOT

French Knot

{1} WRAP FLOSS AROUND NEEDLE: Poke the needle up through the fabric where the knot will be. Wrap the thread around the needle 2 to 5 times, depending on how large you want the knot.

{2} BRING NEEDLE THROUGH WRAPPED FLOSS: Poke the needle straight down next to where the thread came up and pull the wrapped threads snug against the needle while pushing the needle through the fabric, leaving the knot on the surface.

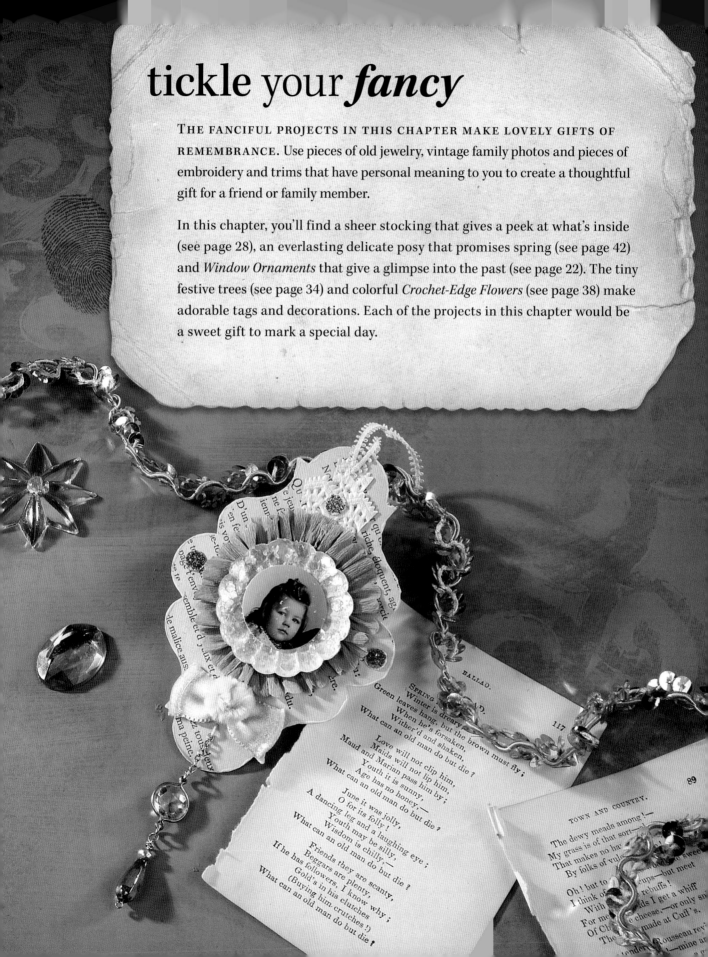

tickle your *fancy*

THE FANCIFUL PROJECTS IN THIS CHAPTER MAKE LOVELY GIFTS OF REMEMBRANCE. Use pieces of old jewelry, vintage family photos and pieces of embroidery and trims that have personal meaning to you to create a thoughtful gift for a friend or family member.

In this chapter, you'll find a sheer stocking that gives a peek at what's inside (see page 28), an everlasting delicate posy that promises spring (see page 42) and *Window Ornaments* that give a glimpse into the past (see page 22). The tiny festive trees (see page 34) and colorful *Crochet-Edge Flowers* (see page 38) make adorable tags and decorations. Each of the projects in this chapter would be a sweet gift to mark a special day.

Joan
1935

window
ornaments

One recent afternoon as my grandmother and I were looking through her photo albums, we came across some charming pictures of my mother as a little girl. I wanted to make a series of ornaments with a winter white palette using old photos of my mother and other family members. A tag hanging from a shirt I purchased from Anthropologie became the inspiration for the first window ornament. I used the tag to outline a shape for the paper base and then used the beautiful but stained old hand-embroidered linens I had collected to decorate around the felt frame and photo.

When hung as a collection, these ornaments are like little windows into another time.

materials

2" × 3" (5cm × 8cm) piece of cream felt

6" (15cm) square of watercolor paper

1 sheet vintage book paper

1 sheet vintage photo album paper

small scraps of embroidered linens
 and lace

5" (13cm) of trim for hanging

small family photo, approximately
 1" × 1½" (3cm × 4cm)

4 glass beads

glitter circles (see page 25)

fine glass glitter

mica flakes

off-white acrylic paint

paintbrush

glue stick

tacky glue

freezer paper

hole punch

scissors

iron

tweezers (optional)

pencil

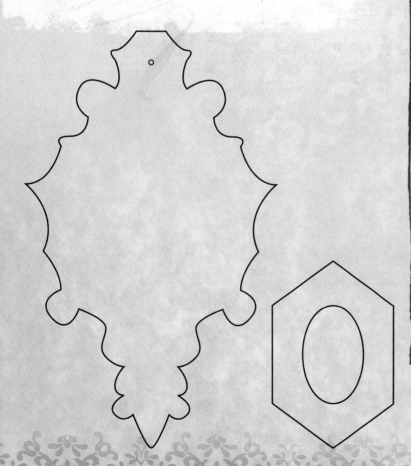

Enlarge ornament and window templates by 125% to bring to actual size.

1 cut out background paper and adhere to cardboard base

Cut out the ornament pattern on page 23 and trace around it onto a piece of watercolor paper. Cut out the ornament shape. Adhere the book paper to the watercolor paper with a glue stick or gel medium and cut it out.

2 paint back and sides of ornament

Paint the back and sides of the ornament with off-white acrylic paint. Let the paint dry. If you like, you may cover the back of the ornament with paper instead of painting it.

3 cut out felt window

Cut out the window pattern on page 23 and trace around it onto a piece of freezer paper. Iron the freezer paper shiny-side down to the felt. Cut out the felt window. Peel away the freezer paper.

4 sprinkle felt window with mica

Spread some tacky glue onto the front of the felt window and sprinkle it with mica flakes. Shake off the excess mica, and allow the glue to dry.

5 *arrange linen and lace pieces*

Lay the felt window on the ornament and cut up small bits of embroidered linens and lace to arrange behind the window, framing it. When you have an arrangement you like, glue the linen and lace pieces to the ornament using tacky glue.

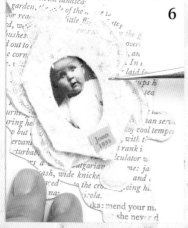

6 *glue photo and frame*

Glue the family photo and the felt window frame in place. Print out the name and date on a piece of vintage photo album paper and glue it in place.

7 *adhere glitter circles and glass beads*

Adhere glass beads and glitter circles to the ornament with small dots of glue. (See the tip on this page for how to make glitter circles.)

TIP

To make a glitter circle, spread a thin layer of tacky glue onto a small piece of cardstock using an old credit card. Sprinkle the glue with fine glass glitter and shake off the excess. Let it dry. Cut out shapes using a hole punch or a decorative punch.

8 *add hanger*

To finish the ornament, fold the 5" (13cm) piece of trim in half and tie a knot in the ends. Thread the loop through the hole, leaving the knot in the back to create the hanger.

more ideas...

Once you have the basic idea down, you can make these ornaments in lots of different shapes and sizes, using different trims. Here are a few more window ornaments to inspire you. Templates for these ornaments are provided on page 27.

1

2

3

baby.

4

5

TIP

Pieces of broken jewelry can be used to make a sparkly dangle.

{1} Delicate embroidery and small sew-on gems frame this photo. A piece of tulle is gathered and glued beneath the felt frame.

{2} Colored floral wallpaper was used for the background on this ornament. A blue ribbon rosette has a glass button center for decoration.

{3} A small piece of acetate was sewn to the back of the felt window before attaching it to this ornament to protect the photo.

{4} A piece of broken chain was used to hang this ornament. The rhinestone necklace clasp at the base of the photograph still has the beading threads attached.

{5} A ruffle of crêpe paper was gathered in a circle beneath a metal cup from a candle clip to frame this small photo.

Enlarge the ornament and window templates by 200% to bring to full size.

holiday
stockings

I enjoy making tiny felt stockings to fill and give as gifts. One afternoon I was searching for a lovely presentation for a gift for my friend Noelle when I came across a bundle of sheer flocked handkerchiefs with beautiful decorative edges I had purchased at an estate sale. I decided to make a sweet stocking that would offer a lovely view of the gift inside. The cream-colored felt created a sturdy base for the stocking that allowed the delicate details of the flocking on the hanky to show through. I used several small scraps of vintage ribbons and trims for the whimsical decoration on the cuff and tied on a small mirror rosette from the hardware store as a final touch. A smaller version of this stocking can be made using paper or felt and filled with little letters and sweets.

materials

cream wool felt

vintage handkerchief

3" (8cm) of trim

4" (10cm) of cording for hanger

8" (20cm) of narrow ribbon or trim

sprig of flowers

wired bullion trim

mirror rosette

button

beads and baubles to go inside stocking

mica flakes

tacky glue

scissors

scallop-edge scissors

sewing machine and thread

sewing needle and thread

straight pins

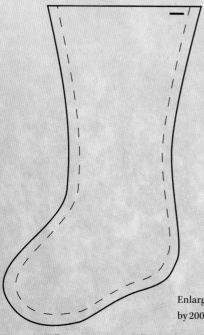

Enlarge the stocking template
by 200% to bring to full size.

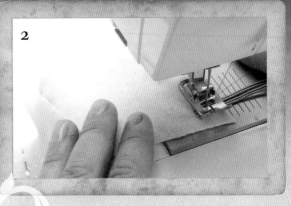

1 cut out front and back of stocking

Lay the stocking pattern on page 29 over a piece of cream-colored felt and cut out the stocking. Place a vintage handkerchief over the cream stocking and fold the edge of the hankie down to create a cuff. Pin the hand-kerchief in place. Cut the handkerchief into a stocking shape using the cream-colored stocking as a guide.

2 create hanger

Fold the cording in half, and use a sewing machine to sew across the ends of the cording to attach a hanger to the cream-colored felt backing.

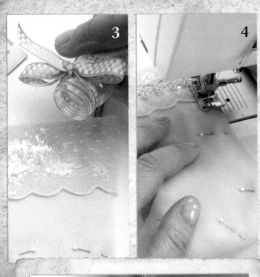

3 add mica and lace trim

Apply a bit of glue to the lacy cuff of the stocking, then sprinkle some mica flakes onto the cuff. While the glue is still wet, adhere a length of lacy trim across the middle of the cuff. Allow the glue to dry.

4 seam pieces together

Pin together the 2 stockings and sew around the edges with a ¼" (6mm) seam.

5 cut scalloped edge

Trim the edge of the stocking with scallop-edge scissors.

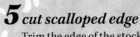

6 add decorations

Thread a narrow piece of ribbon through a bead or button, then pull the ends of the ribbon through the central opening of a mirror rosette. Tie the ribbon ends in a knot to secure the bead flower center in place. Layer a piece of bullion and a sprig of flowers under the mirror rosette. Use a sewing needle and thread to secure the decoration to 1 corner of the stocking.

7 *add beads to stocking*

Slip a selection of beads into the toe of the stocking as a final decorative touch.

another idea...

A lovely flower was used in place of a mirror rosette for this sweet stocking variation.

more
ideas...

tiny stocking tags

Use the patterns below to make smaller versions of the larger stockings. Hang them on a miniature tree or tie them to gifts with a little note tucked inside.

Sew together two stockings cut from felt or paper and decorate the tops with small pieces of felt, bells, paper lace or mica. Add a tiny string hanger to the side for hanging.

Enlarge the template for the tiny stocking tags by 150% to bring to full size.

skinny stockings

Vintage book papers were used to make these two skinny stockings. The book paper can be brushed with matte gel medium to strengthen it, if desired, or brushed with a wash of watered-down acrylic paint to add color. Glue a loop of string or trim to the stocking before adding the cuff. The cuffs were made using crêpe paper and felt, then decorated before being glued to the sewn paper stockings. Follow the directions on page 25 for making your own glitter circles.

Enlarge the template for the skinny stocking by 200% to bring to full size.

christmas
trees

The first felt Christmas trees I made were little tags on my holiday gifts. I had so much fun selecting the trims and sewing together the felt and paper. It was a great way to use even the tiniest bit of leftover vintage trim too pretty to throw away. You can change the look of each tree by using a variety of buttons, trims and paper flowers. Add some glass garland beads and a sprinkle of glass glitter or mica flakes for a bit of sparkle.

materials

vintage book page

thin chipboard or watercolor paper

small pieces of patterned paper

small piece of pink wool felt

vintage handkerchief with scalloped edge

string

silver thread

several beads

silver star

glitter circles (see page 25)

fine glass glitter

mica flakes

glue stick

tacky glue

scallop-edge scissors

scissors

flower punch

circle template

tweezers

pencil

Enlarge the templates for the Christmas trees by 200% to bring to full size.

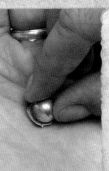

1 trace template

Cut out the tree pattern provided on page 35. Trace around the tree onto a piece of book paper twice. Cut out 2 trees. Trace and cut out a third tree from watercolor paper. Adhere 1 book paper tree to each side of the cardboard tree with a glue stick. Spread a thin layer of glue onto the front of the tree and shake on some mica flakes. Set the tree aside to dry.

2 begin to make cupped paper flowers

Punch several flower shapes from patterned paper using a flower punch. Place a paper flower into the palm of your hand and press a bead into the paper, creating a flower that is cupped around the bead.

3 make felt ornament

Trace small circles onto pink pieces of felt using the circle template. Cut just outside of the lines with scallop-edge scissors. Turn the felt circles so the pen line is on the back.

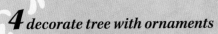

4 decorate tree with ornaments

Glue some glitter circles to the centers of the felt circles. Glue these layered circles to the front of the tree. Also glue the cupped paper flowers to the tree, carefully gluing a bead into the center of each one. Allow the glue to dry.

5 cut out tree trunk

Cut a piece of the scalloped edge off a vintage handkerchief to create the tree trunk. Glue the trunk in place, and allow the glue to dry.

6 add glitter star and hanger to tree top

Spread some glue onto a silver star and liberally apply fine glass glitter. Let the star dry. Cut a loop of string and glue it in place under the star at the top of the tree.

7 tie silver thread around tree trunk

Cut 2 short lengths of silver thread and tie them around the trunk of the tree.

more ideas...

You can make little trees any way you like.

{1} Pick a color palette and glue several trims in those shades to a felt background.

{2} Glue thin string and beads to your paper tree for a festive garland. Or use a thicker yarn and leave off the beads.

{3} A tiny tree sparkles in a cellophane bag of vintage mica snow as a gift from my friend Candice Elton.

crochet-edge
flowers

Thick wool felt has a wonderful feel and looks great paired with glass beads and stitching. This crochet-edge flower requires no hole punching for the crochet hook and is easy to whip up in about ten minutes once you've learned the technique. Embroider a wool bead or use a vintage beaded earring for the center of your felt flower. Sew your funky flowers to little clip barrettes, or use them to decorate a favorite purse. Try a wool yarn instead of the pearl cotton thread for a really funky look!

materials

2" to 3" (5cm to 8cm) square of wool felt (thick, tight felt works best)

size 10 crochet hook

size 8 DMC pearl cotton thread

embroidery floss and needle

vintage clip-on earring

E6000 (optional)

freezer paper

scissors

wire cutters

iron

pencil

Flower template shown at actual size.

1 cut out flower

Trace the flower pattern on this page onto a piece of freezer paper. Iron the freezer paper shiny-side down onto a piece of felt. Cut out the flower shape, and peel away the freezer paper.

2 begin crochet border

Poke the tip of the crochet hook through the felt at the base of one of the petals about 1/8" (3mm) in from the edge and pull through a loop of cotton pearl thread.

3 pull thread through loop

Wrap the thread connected to the ball over the crochet hook counterclockwise, and pull the thread through the loop.

4 draw up next loop

Poke the crochet hook through the felt again at a point 1/8" (3mm) from the starting point and pull a loop through. There are now 2 loops of thread on your hook, as shown.

5 bring thread through both loops

Wrap the thread over the crochet hook counterclockwise, and pull the thread through both loops. Repeat steps 2 through 5 around the flower until you are back to the first stitch, always poking the tip of the crochet hook through the felt about 1/8" (3mm) from the previous stitch when beginning a new stitch.

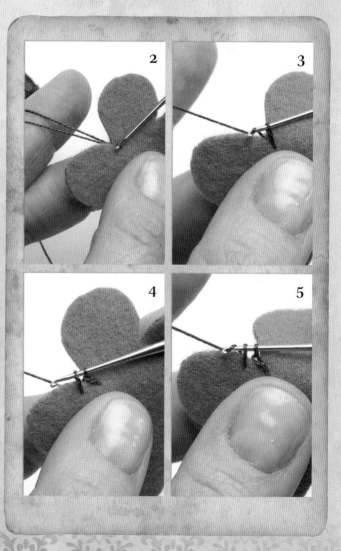

6 secure thread

Poke the crochet needle back through the first stitch, wrap the thread over the crochet hook and pull the thread through both loops. Cut the thread 3" (8cm) from the hook, pull the thread end through the loop and pull snug.

7 knot threads to secure border

Tie a square knot at the back of the flower with the 2 ends, and tuck the ends through 2 stitches on the back. Clip the ends of the threads.

8 cut off back of clip-on earring

Use wire cutters to clip off the back of the clip-on earring.

9 sew earring to flower center

Thread an embroidery needle with embroidery thread and tie a knot in the end. Bring the needle up through the center of the flower and through 1 of the holes in the earring. Bring the needle back down through another hole and to the back of the flower. Continue stitching until the earring is firmly attached to the flower. Then tie off the thread and clip the ends. If the earring you're using doesn't have any holes to sew through, glue it in place with E6000.

more ideas...

Embellish all sorts of things with these simple flowers.

1

2

3

{1} To make flowers like these, follow the instructions on page 89 to make an embroidered felt bead center.

{2} At the center of the beautiful treasure box above by Kristin Steiner and Susan Edmonson is this layered and embroidered felt flower with an unusual metal frame center.

{3} A sparkling rhinestone-and-green-bead earring dresses up the center of a wool tweed flower with black crocheted edging. The felt flower is surrounded by velvet leaves, wrapped berries and netting. It adds an elegant touch to this vintage purse.

wire-wrapped

posy

As my collection of old millinery flowers grows I am continually surprised by the uniqueness of each flower design. The wire-wrapped posy uses wool felt for the petals of these flowers inspired by vintage millinery bouquets. Wire bullion is sewn around the felt and hides the wire that shapes the petals. These wire-wrapped flowers make a sweet posy or decorate a delicate powder box to hold your favorite trinkets.

materials

small piece of pink wool felt

variety of silk leaves and buds

4 pearl beads from a broken vintage necklace

32-gauge wire

28-gauge wire

wired bullion trim

scraps of narrow ribbons or lace

small piece of tulle or netting

florist's tape

wire cutters

scissors

needle and thread

1 *thread bullion onto wire*
Cut a 6" (15cm) length of 28-gauge wire. Cut a ¾" (2cm) piece of bullion and thread it onto the middle of the wire.

2 *stretch bullion*
Carefully stretch the bullion in each direction until it covers 1½" (4cm) of the center of the wire.

3 twist wire into petal shape

Shape the bullion-covered wire into a petal. Twist the ends of the wire together to hold the petal shape.

4 sew petal to felt square

Cut a small square of felt to fit under the petal shape. Using a sewing needle and thread the same color as the felt, stitch around the bullion-covered petal to secure it to the felt, beginning at the base of the petal and hiding the knot at the back of the felt square. Stitch around the wire, pulling the thread snug to hold the petal in place on the felt. As you stitch, make sure the thread falls between the coils of the bullion and rests on the wire petal form. Continue making small stitches all the way around the petal.

5 cut felt into petal shape

After stitching all the way around the petal and securing the wire at the base of the petal on both sides, tie off the thread at the back of the felt and trim the thread close to the knot. Carefully trim away the excess felt around the wired petal, making sure not to cut through the stitching threads. Repeat to make 4 more petals. Shape each petal in a slight convex shape by gently bending the wire frame. Set the petals aside.

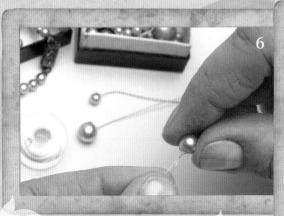

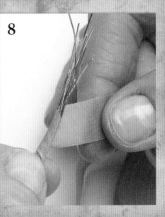

6 make beaded stamens

Cut a 4" (10cm) piece of 32-gauge wire, and thread a pearl bead from a broken vintage necklace onto the center of the wire. Fold the wire in half and twist the ends together in an even twist up to the bead. Make 4 more beaded stamens. Use 1 larger pearl and 4 smaller ones.

7 secure with wire

Gather the stamens and the petals together, keeping the stamens in the center of the flower. Cut a 7" (18cm) length of 28-gauge wire and wrap it tightly around the base of the flower to secure it. Clip off the wire ends.

8 wrap stems in florist's tape

Wrap the bundled wire stem with florist's tape, beginning at the base of the flower and continuing until the wires are entirely covered.

9 make posy

Gather some silk leaves and buds and bits of tulle or netting, and arrange them around the flower into a posy.

10 add decorative bow

When you are happy with your arrangement, secure the posy by tying short pieces of ribbon or lace around the stems.

another idea...

Cover a vintage powder box with papers and ribbon. Then glue small flowers and buds around the top of the lid, adding a wire-wrapped flower in the center.

nooks & crannies

TAKE A CAREFUL LOOK AT EACH OF THE PROJECTS IN THIS CHAPTER—
YOU'LL FIND SOMETHING UNEXPECTED INSIDE EVERY ONE. A little book decorated inside and out with bits of felt holds a quiet story (see page 58). A treasury of
needles nestles inside the warm felt pages of a needle book (see page 52), and the word
"peace" graces the cover of a repurposed bound book (see page 48). Little pouches
hold their contents snug for traveling inside an *iPod Sweater* (see page 62), behind
a vintage zipper (see page 70), and tied carefully with a piece of lace (see page 66).

You'll find new uses for all sorts of unusual materials in this chapter, including a
metal screen from the hardware store, a paper needle book and a single vintage
earring. All of these misfit materials are repurposed into useful and fanciful items
you'll use every day.

a secret

[in the garden]

TIP

Next time you discard an old self-healing mat, cut out a small rectangle to fit inside your travel tool kit. The small piece fits inside a book and protects the pages while you are cutting, drilling or making holes with a Japanese screw punch.

window
book

A tiny worn book with a decorated cover came home with me one day after a thrift-store shopping trip. The pale gray-blue looked so wintry, I decided to make a book for recording the peacefulness of being tucked under a blanket of white snow for the winter. Pale gray-blue, cream and silver became the palette as I selected a small scrap of wool felt, silver-lined glass beads and a wintry paper poinsettia. The embroidered felt and glittered flower peek through the small window in the cover of the book, sparkling like the blanket of white outside my window.

Peace

Enlarge the window cut-out and embroidery template by 150% to bring to full size.

materials

small hardcover thrift-store book

*small rectangle of cream wool felt
   (to fit behind window)*

decorative paper or wallpaper

18 glass silver-lined E beads

German scrap flower

floral stamens

wired bullion trim

silver glass glitter

flake glitter or mica flakes

silver DMC embroidery floss and needle

repositionable tape

tacky glue

craft knife

self-healing cutting mat

straightedge

pencil

drill and ³⁄₃₄" (2mm) drill bit

block of wood

scissors

1 cut rectangle out of book cover

Draw a rectangle on the cover of the small book for a window. My book is 6" × 4" (15cm × 10cm) and the size of the window is 1⅞" × 2¾" (5cm × 7cm). Make adjustments in the size of the window to fit your book. Open the book so the front cover rests on a self-healing cutting mat. With a craft knife and straightedge, cut along the penciled lines. Use a fresh blade and don't try to cut clear through the cover all at once. Make several cuts along the same line, each time going a bit deeper until your blade cuts through.

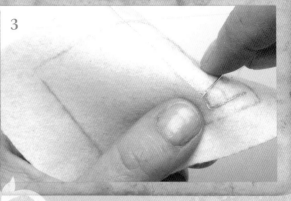

2 trace inside window onto felt

Remove the cut piece from the center of the book. Place a piece of felt under the front cover. Using a pencil, lightly trace around the window. Trim the piece of felt, leaving ¾" (2cm) extending along each side. Use a pencil to lightly draw the letters for the word you want to embroider.

3 embroider letters

Thread one strand of silver floss onto an embroidery needle and tie a knot at the end of the floss. Poke the needle Through the back of the felt at the end of the first letter, leaving the knot at the back of the felt. Outline each of the letters with a stem stitch. (See page 18 for instructions on working a stem stitch.)

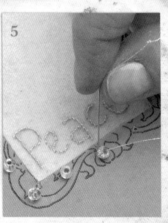

TIP

The silver embroidery floss is quite fragile. Don't unpick the thread and reuse it. Watch the thread for cracking near the eye of the needle.

4 drill holes in cover

Use a pencil to mark the placement of the holes where the glass beads will be sewn on the cover. Open the book and lay the front cover on top of a block of wood. Use a ¾" (2mm) bit to drill the holes.

5 sew on beads

Tape the felt rectangle to the back of the cover with repositionable tape, centering the embroidered word(s) in the window. Tie a knot at the end of 1 strand of silver floss, and starting on the wrong side of the felt, poke the needle through the felt and through a hole in the cover. String on 1 E bead, and poke the needle back down the same hole in the cover. Pull the floss snug. Poke the needle up through the felt at the next hole in the cover. Repeat until all the beads are sewn in place. Tie a knot after the last bead, and trim the floss.

6 apply mica flakes

Trim the connecting edges of the German scrap flower. Use your finger to spread a thin film of tacky glue over the edges of the petals. Dust the flower with flake glitter or mica, and shake off the excess.

7 glitter stamens

Dip the ends of several stamens into a bit of tacky glue, then roll them in silver glass glitter. Allow them to dry.

8 insert stamens through center of flower

Poke several holes through the center of the flower with a needle. Poke a floral stamen through each hole. Gather the stamen ends to the back. Hold the stamen ends in place and wrap a thread around them close to the flower several times. Tie a knot in the thread and clip the ends. Trim away the ends of the stamens.

9 adhere flower to front of book

Apply a dot of tacky glue to the back of the flower to hold the stamens in place. Adhere a couple of glittered stamens and strands of bullion to the back of the flower. Glue the finished flower in the window.

10 add decorative paper to inside of cover

Trim a piece of decorative paper or a bit of sturdy wallpaper to fit inside the front cover of the book. Glue the paper in place with tacky glue to stabilize the felt and cover the stitching.

needle
book

I came across an old sewing box at an estate sale one afternoon filled with wooden spools of thread, old snap cards and zippers, and little pill bottles filled with different colors of old buttons. There were many little goodies tucked away in the corners of the sewing box, but the paper needle book caught my attention right away. I enjoy sewing by hand, but I do not enjoy the search for the right size needle. I decided right then I would make a needle book so I could organize my pins and embroidery needles on soft felt pages so I could find them easily.

Images of the women who taught me to craft, my mother, Joan, and grandmother Eloise, are sewed onto the pages in my needle book. Many times my mother would sew late into the night making doll outfits for me and my sisters to open Christmas morning, as well as fancy dresses for dances and concerts. My grandmother gave me my first craft kit and taught me to crochet, and I have been busy making things ever since.

materials

black, light pink, dark pink, green
   and blue wool felt

sturdy new or vintage paper needle book

piece of narrow ribbon or fibers
   to bind book

small beads

embroidery floss in colors to coordinate
   with the felt and embroidery needle

scraps of lace and bits of jewelry

freezer paper

appliqué pins

large-eyed needle

quilter's pencil

pinking shears

large-eyed needle

scissors

iron

Enlarge the templates for the flowers and vase by 150% to bring to full size.

1 cut and fold cover and inside pages

Cut 1 piece of black felt to 9" × 6" (23cm × 15cm) for the cover. Fold the cover in half and press it. Cut 1 piece of pink felt to 8¾" × 5⅞" (22cm × 15cm) for the inside pages. Fold this smaller square in half and press it. Cut around the edges of the smaller square with pinking shears.

2 cut out floral design

Trace the design for the vase, flowers, stems and leaves on page 53 onto the matte side of a piece of freezer paper. Cut out the shapes and iron them onto the felt pieces with the shiny side of the freezer paper against the felt. Cut out the felt shapes, and gently peel off the freezer paper.

3 pin vase and flowers onto cover

Lay the pieces for the vase, stems, leaves and flowers on the cover of the needle book. Pin all the pieces in place.

4 begin stitching vase and flowers in place

Begin stitching the stems in place, using a coordinating color of thread and working a blanket stitch around the edges. (See page 19 for instructions on working a blanket stitch.) After all 3 stems are sewn in place, stitch on the leaves and then stitch around the vase. Make sure the vase overlaps the bottom of the flower stems by ⅜" (1cm). Stitch the petals and center of the central flower in place.

6 add decorative embroidery and beading

Draw the lines for the embroidered flower stems with a quilter's pencil, and stitch along the lines using a stem stitch. Add the embroidered leaves using a daisy stitch. (See pages 18 and 19 for instructions on working a stem stitch and a daisy stitch, respectively.) Stitch on a few seed beads, following the curves of the stitched stems to create tiny buds.

5 embellish flowers

Sew the felt flowers in place and embellish them with bits of broken jewelry or lace.

TIP

To cut out the light pink and blue flowers, lay a circle template on the back side of your felt. Trace a $^{13}/_{16}$" (21mm) circle lightly with pencil. Cut around the circle with zigzag- or scallop-edge shears, cutting along the pencil line.

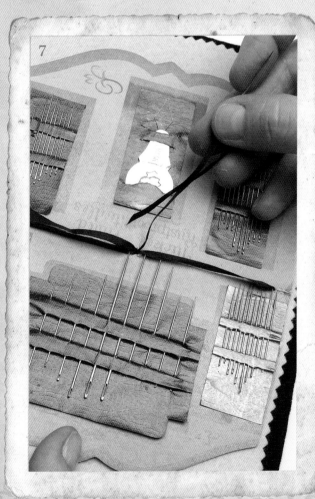

7 make holes for assembly

Open the cover of the book and center the inside page in place. Open the needle book and center it on top of the felt page. Mark a center hole and a hole ⅜" (1cm) from each end of the paper needle book. Thread some narrow ribbon or fibers onto a large-eyed needle. With the book open, poke the needle down through the bottom hole, leaving a long tail. Then poke the needle up through the cover and pages through the top hole. Bring the needle down through the center hole and slip the needle off the ribbon. Thread the needle onto the bottom ribbon, and again poke the needle through the center hole and pull the ribbons snug. Tie the 2 ends of the ribbon on the outside of the book. Or, for a tie on the inside of the book, tie a square knot on the outside of the book, and thread both ribbons on the needle and poke them back through the center hole to the inside and tie. Trim the ribbon ends.

The paper needle book is the cover of this
little sewing kit. To make one of your own,
glue a piece of felt to the outside of the needle
book to reinforce the fold. Sew a second piece
of felt inside the needle book along the fold
and attach a narrow ribbon to hold a pair of
embroidery scissors in place.

scissors

B**ONITA**
TRADE MARK · REG. U.S. PAT. OFF.
NEEDLES

This needle book is made using three pieces of felt folded in half and stitched together with fibers. To make the cover, sew several ribbons and trims onto a piece of felt, then embellish it with glass seed beads and a velvet flower. I copied photos of my family onto a sheet of t-shirt transfer paper, then ironed the transfers onto fabric and stitched them to the felt pages. Decorate the pages where the pins and needles are kept with trims and embroidery.

Two Art Girls
sheila julie
1969

quiet

book

I am the mother of four active children, and one day I realized my days had become too busy and noisy. I started hiding out in my studio, hoping for a quiet moment, and that's when I began working on the *Quiet Book*. The metal screen came in a huge piece from my hardware store. It had many small holes in the metal to sew through, and when combined with the felt squares it made an unusual textured cover for my book.

My daughter Olivia began coming downstairs to check on my progress each day, and she started suggesting things I should use in the book. She learned to read the words on each page as I worked, and when "her book" was completed she said to me, "Now I want you to make me a *loud* book."

materials

metal screen

wool felt in various colors

fabric scraps

cotton quilt batting (optional)

a selection of buttons

an old book or dictionary

embroidery floss

approximately 30″ (76cm) of ribbon

4 beads with large holes for binding

matte gel medium

little bits to decorate pages, including ribbon, feathers, buttons, yarn, appliqués, ricrac, beads, shells, bits of old hankies, lace, pictures, photos, pins, charms, fabric bits

sewing needle and thread

assorted needles

drill and small bit

tin snips or metal sheers

punch

small hammer

iron

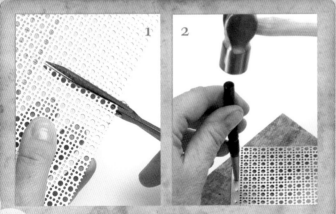

1 cut metal screen

Cut 2 pieces of metal screen to 3½" × 2½" (9cm × 6cm) for the front and back covers of the book using tin snips or metal shears. Sand or spray paint the metal, if desired.

2 make indents in metal screen to mark hole placement

Use a punch and a small hammer to make 5 evenly spaced indents in each piece of metal screen ⅛" (3mm) from the edge. These indentions keep the drill from sliding around and help you create precise holes. Use a drill with a small bit to make a hole at each indented mark for both the front and back covers.

3

4

4 *baste pages together*

Baste all the pages together along the left-hand side using a sewing needle and thread to hold the pages in place so they won't move around as you bind the book.

3 *create pages*

Cut 5 felt pages the same size as the cover and 2 fabric pages to 2½" × 7" (6cm × 18cm). Fold the fabric pages in half and press them. Sandwich a single layer of 3½" × 2½" (9cm × 6cm) cotton quilt batting inside the folded fabric page if the fabric is thin. Stack the pages and covers of the book in the order in which you'd like them to appear in the book.

5

6

7

5 *collage book title onto button*

Cut words from an old book or dictionary to spell out the title of your book. Use matte gel medium to collage the words onto a large button. Allow the gel medium to dry.

6 *embellish cover*

Cut small squares of assorted felt and fabric, and select a variety of small buttons, 1 to sew on each square. Cut a larger square of fabric to go in the middle of the cover and sew it in place. Sew the large central button on top of the fabric square, stitching through the fabric and metal screen. Arrange the remaining fabric and felt squares on the cover, and sew them in place. Stitch the buttons in place on top of the fabric and felt squares, stitching through the holes in the metal screen and through each felt or fabric square.

7 *begin binding book*

Sandwich the basted pages between the front and back covers of the book. Begin sewing the book together with a 14" (36cm) length of ribbon threaded through a needle. Bring the needle down through the first hole on the front cover, through the fabric pages, and then through the first hole in the back cover of the book. String a bead onto the ribbon, then bring the ribbon down through the next hole in the front of the book. Continue threading the ribbon through the holes in the cover and threading on beads until you reach the final hole in the back cover.

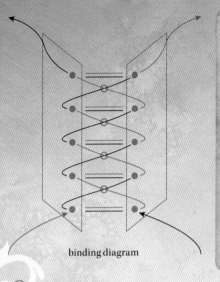

binding diagram

8 *finish binding*

Thread a second 14" (36cm) piece of ribbon on a needle, and thread the needle through the bottom hole across from where the first ribbon finished. Crisscross the ribbon through each bead, working from the bottom up to the top. See the diagram on this page for specific binding instructions.

9 *secure ribbons*

After both ribbons have been threaded through the book, tie a small bow at each end and trim the ribbon.

inside pages...

Use pieces of ribbon, printed fabric or lace to create a background on your felt pages. Use words cut from old books or embroidery to add text to your little collages. Add beads, buttons, feathers and stitching to create texture and interest.

iPod

sweater

Sometimes one item inspires an entire project. I found a darling child's sweater that had charming colors and a darling picot trim at the hem for fifty cents at a thrift store. It had already been accidentally felted when it was washed—perfect for me!

I was excited to try making a little sweater pocket for my daughter, hoping to extend the life of her new iPod. The little iPod sweater is soft and snug, small enough for her to tuck into her jeans pocket or in her purse—and off she goes.

materials

thrift store 100% wool sweater

green wool roving

green wool felt

green embroidery floss

embroidery needle

needle-felting needle

needle-felting foam

scissors

sewing machine and thread

Template for the iPod sweater shown at actual size.

1 cut out iPod sweater front and back

Look for a 100% wool sweater at a thrift shop in a color and pattern you like. Wash the sweater in hot water with detergent in the washing machine, and dry it in the dryer to felt the fibers and shrink the sweater. Copy the pattern for the iPod sweater on page 63 and lay it on the sweater with the top of the pattern lined up with the hem. Cut out 2 sweater pieces.

2 begin needle felting flower

Lay the front piece down on a piece of needle-felting foam. Pull out a piece of green roving and lay it on the sweater for the flower stem, following the pattern. Begin felting the roving to the sweater by poking the felting needle down through the roving and sweater into the foam.

3 needle felt flower center and petals

Continue poking the needle through the green roving along the sides and through the middle until the wool is in a firm design against the sweater. Pull out a small bit of wool roving for the flower center. Roll it into a smooth ball and lay it in place on the sweater. Needle felt the flower center and petals to the sweater using the pattern as a guide.

4 *sew on leaves*

Cut 2 green leaves from green wool felt and back-stitch them to the stem, using embroidery floss. (See page 18 for instructions on working a backstitch.)

5 *backstitch around petals*

Backstitch around the stem, flower center and petals to outline them, using all 6 strands of embroidery floss.

6 *sew front and back together*

Lay the 2 sweater pieces right sides together and sew around three sides of the sweater, leaving the top open. Sew around the sweater a second time just outside your first stitching line. Trim away the excess seam allowance close to the second line of stitching, and turn the sweater right side out. Slip your iPod inside to test for a snug fit. Adjust the seam allowance, if necessary.

jewelry
envelope

I always wear earrings—they are my favorite jewelry. One day I was getting ready for a trip and packed the earrings I was taking in a plastic bag. I wished I had a wool envelope instead—what a lovely way for my favorite earrings to travel. This jewelry envelope is a simple rectangle with a pocket that folds up and closes with a single vintage earring over the lace tie. This small project is all stitched by hand—tuck it in your purse and relax by working on it whenever you have a few minutes of waiting. Or design a wool felt envelope to wrap a small gift for a beautiful presentation.

materials

wool felt

vintage earring

approximately 12" (30cm) of sheer lace ribbon

embroidery floss and needle

approxmiately 6" (15cm) of lace trim

enough rayon seam binding or narrow ribbon to go around the perimeter of the envelope

jewelry pliers

tacky glue

scissors

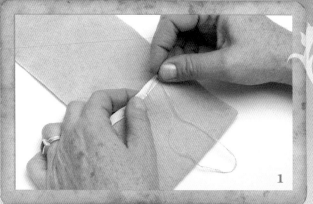

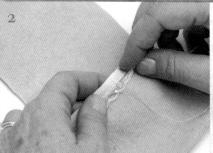

1 cut out envelope, press into shape and sew binding in place

Cut a rectangle of felt 4" (10cm) wide and 12½" (32cm) long. Cut 1 end of the rectangle into an envelope flap, following the pattern on this page. On the opposite end, fold up the bottom 3" (8cm) to form a pocket and press it. Cut a 4½" (11cm) length of ⁹⁄₁₆" (14mm) wide ribbon or rayon seam binding and press it in half. Fold the seam binding over the top edge of the pocket and pin it in place. With a single strand of embroidery floss, sew along the seam binding with a small running stitch. (See page 18 for instructions on working a running stitch.) Trim the ends of the floss and seam binding carefully.

2 sew lace

Sew a narrow piece of lace directly beneath the seam binding.

3 sew seam binding along envelope edges

Fold up the pocket and pin it in place. Cut 24" (61cm) of seam binding and press it in half. Fold the end of the seam binding in ¼" (6mm) to enclose the cut end of the ribbon, and, starting at the bottom edge of the pocket, fold the seam binding over the edge of the pouch. Sew the seam binding in place with a tiny running stitch. Check the stitching as you sew to be sure the thread catches evenly on both sides. When you reach the point at the flap, make a small tuck and sew it in place. When you reach the end of the envelope, trim the seam binding, leaving ¼" (6mm) to fold inside. Sew the ends of the seam binding in place. Tie off the embroidery floss and trim away the excess.

Enlarge the jewelry envelope template to 175% to bring to full size.

4 finish envelope

Fold the envelope. Cut a narrow piece of sheer lace ribbon 18" (46cm) long. wrap it around the envelope and tie it in a bow at the center of the flap. Trim the ends of the lace.

Use the jewelry pliers to carefully pull the clip back off an old earring, and glue the earring in place above the lace bow. With one strand of floss, tack the lace to the back of the envelope.

another idea...

This jewelry envelope was made using the same pattern as the main project. Finish the edges of the pouch with blanket stitch instead of using seam binding to get a different look. Set a small eyelet into the flap and slip a thin ribbon through the opening to tie the envelope closed.

zipper

purse

I created the zipper purse to contain the stash of little things that was always rattling around at the bottom of my bag: lipstick, gum, fingernail file, coins. I have made several of these little felt purses in different sizes, and they are perfect to hold art pencils, a little first aid kit in the car and my daughter's collection of lip gloss.

The large bead makes a funky zipper pull that's easy to grab. If you want to line the purse with a colorful cotton fabric, baste it to the felt before cutting the scallop edges and sewing in the zipper.

materials

8" × 6½" (20cm × 17cm) piece
    of wool felt

vintage metal zipper

bead and jump ring

button with a shank

scrap of ½" (1cm) wide ricrac or trim

embroidery floss and needle

sewing needle and thread

straight pins

scallop-edge scissors

point turner

wire cutters

flat-nose pliers

sewing machine and thread

iron

Enlarge template for zipper purse
by 150% to bring to actual size.

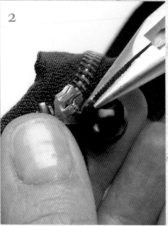

1 remove original zipper pull
Clip off the metal zipper pull using wire cutters.

2 attach bead to zipper
Attach a bead to the zipper with a large jump ring.

3 scallop short edges
Cut a felt rectangle to 8"× 6½" (20cm × 17cm). Scallop the short edges of the felt with scallop-edge scissors.

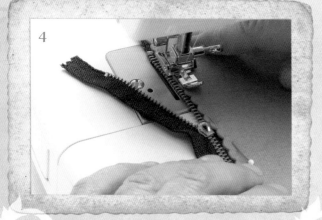

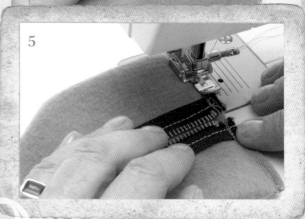

4 pin zipper to scalloped edge and sew
Pin 1 scalloped edge to the zipper, leaving ⅜" (1cm) seam allowance at the top of the zipper. Sew along the top of the felt piece with a zipper foot on your sewing machine.

5 sew pouch sides
Pin the other scalloped edge to the other side of the zipper. Unzip the zipper, and sew the felt along the zipper edge. Zip up the zipper, and turn the purse inside out. Center the zipper evenly down the middle and pin the ends. Sew the top edge first next to the zipper pull. Stitch a ⅜" (1cm) seam close to the zipper. Unzip the zipper a bit, then sew the bottom seam, carefully sewing through the zipper teeth. Stitch over the top and bottom seams a second time, ⅛" (3mm) from the first line of stitching. Trim the threads and the zipper ends, carefully cutting the zipper fabric, not the zipper teeth.

6 make rosette flower

Unzip the purse and turn it inside out, using a point turner for the corners. Zip up the zipper, and press the purse flat. To make the gathered flower, baste a running stitch along an edge of a 3" (8cm) piece of ½" (1cm) wide ricrac or trim. Pull the thread to gather the trim in a rosette, and sew the ends together.

7 sew on rosette flower

Sew the rosette to the pouch with a button center.

8 embellish pouch with embroidered flowers

Embellish the zipper purse with embroidered flowers and polka dots. Refer to the template on page 71 for the placement of the flower and embellishments.

another idea...

Make a zipper purse with cotton fabric and a cotton lining, then use felt for the zipper pull and the flower decorations.

beads & baubles

I LOVE THE FEMININE TEXTURE AND INDUSTRIAL LOOK CREATED BY COMBINING WOOL FELT AND METAL JEWELRY ELEMENTS. My first felt jewelry piece was the result of a winter charm exchange I did with four friends I met at an artists' retreat. I had been experimenting with wool beads and decided to use felt as the medium for my charms. You can see the results of our collaboration on page 76.

This chapter is a collection of techniques for making tiny stuffed and rolled felt baubles embellished with beads and stitching that will be wonderful additions to your own jewelry pieces. Soft, colorful wool beads stitched with glass beads make fanciful rings (see page 88) and necklaces (see page 84). Simple multicolor stacks and rolls of felt are cut into tiny beads that make perfect charms (see page 80). Start with the projects here; then take your beads and make any kind of jewelry you like.

FEATURED ARTISTS

SHERRI HAAB: *polymer clay-and-resin deer charm*

WENDY WALLIN-MALLINOW: *metal clay starfish, pearl and crystal charms*

ADRIENNE KEITH: *white bead charms*

JULIE COLLINGS: *felt cone and felt ornament ball, metal clay leaves, cupped flowers and textured metal clay balls*

felt charm *bracelet*

This charm bracelet is the collection of winter charms I exchanged with three of my artist friends. I wanted to use felt in an unusual way to create my winter-themed charms. The felt cone bead was made using a thin bonded felt that works best for stuffed beads because the felt has a clean edge when cut. The ornament ball is shaped using wool roving fibers and a wet-felting technique to create the ball; then beads and decorative threads are added. A tiny silver bell sewn at the bottom tinkles a bit when I wear my bracelet. The felt baubles are sewn to rings so they can be attached with a separate jump ring to the bracelet base. A soldered head pin is used with the metal beads and charms to form a wire loop at the top of the charm for connecting to the bracelet with a jump ring.

materials

small pieces of felt in coordinating colors

thin, compact cream felt

cream wool roving

seed beads in various colors

various trims, including ricrac and silver trim

polyester fiberfill

6¼" (16cm) large linked chain

5½" (14cm) small linked chain

jump rings

closed rings

*assorted beads and charms,
        including a small silver bell*

embroidery floss and beading needle

craft bond multipurpose spray adhesive (Elmer's)

scissors

freezer paper

Japanese screw punch with ⅛" (3mm) tip

sewing needle and thread

straightedge

circle template (optional)

rotary cutter and cutting mat

appliqué pins

straight pins

iron

cone bead

1

1 cut out pieces for cone bead

Trace the patterns on page 126 onto freezer paper and iron them shiny side down onto a small piece of felt. Cut out the 2 pieces.

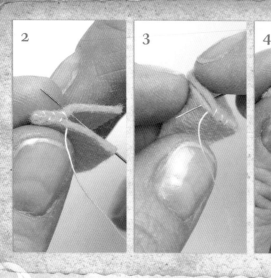

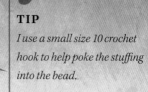

2 sew bead into cone shape

Use a needle and matching thread to sew the 2 straight edges together to form a cone.

3 sew cone to base

Pin the circle on the bottom of the cone in 2 places with tiny appliqué pins. Sew ¾ of the way around the circle.

4 stuff cone

Stuff the cone bead with polyester fiberfill. When the shape is nicely filled out, continue sewing around the circle to close the cone.

5 make felt circles

Using a ⅛" (3mm) tip in a Japanese screw punch, make 10 to 12 tiny felt circles from a thin, compact cream-colored felt.

6 sew felt circles and beads onto cone

Thread a beading needle with a single strand of embroidery floss. Tie a knot in the end of the thread and hide the knot inside the cone bead. Poke the needle up where you want to attach a bead. Bring the needle through the center of a felt circle and then through a bead and back down through the center of the felt circle and into the felt cone. Poke your needle out at the next place for a felt circle and bead. Continue adding little felt circles and beads around the cone until you like the placement.

7 sew jump ring to top of cone bead

Poke your needle through the point of the cone. Thread on a ⅛" (3mm) round silver bead and a closed silver ring. Sew the ring securely in place. Tie off and clip the thread. Attach the felt cone to a charm bracelet with a jump ring.

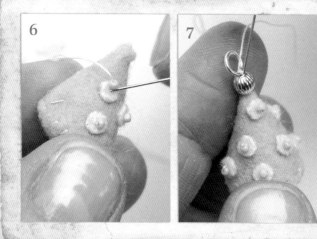

ornament ball

1 *begin to make ornament ball*

Felt a cream-colored round wool bead to a finished size of ¾" (2cm). (See pages 16–17 for instructions on making a felted ball.) Sew a piece of narrow silver trim around the ball in 2 overlapping circles to divide the ball into quarters, using a straight pin to anchor the trim in place as you sew. Make small stitches through the silver trim, poking the needle through the trim to anchor it to the felt ball.

2 *sew on blue beads*

Sew glass seed beads around the felt ball using a needle and thread, taking tiny stitches to secure the beads to the ball.

3 *sew bell to felt ball*

Sew a small silver bell to the bottom of the felt ball.

4 *sew on jump ring*

Poke the needle through the ball out the top and through a silver-lined clear glass E bead and around a closed silver ring. Secure the ring with thread, tie it off and clip the thread. Use a jump ring to attach the felt ornament to the charm bracelet.

You can dream up all sorts of felt beads. Roll
up two contrasting colors of felt and slice them
into beads. Make a thick, colorful stack of felt
and cut out tiny squares to embellish. Or make
a felt sushi roll and chop it up to make beads
with multicolored insides. Maybe you'll dream
up your own original felt bead design.

bundled bead

1 glue layers together

Cut 5 small rectangles of felt in different colors and stack them in an order you like. Working outside or in a well-ventilated area, spray the bottom layer with multi-purpose adhesive and press the next layer on top. Continue to spray each layer until the whole stack is adhered together. Allow the glue to dry.

2 cut the sandwich into small squares

Use a straightedge and a rotary cutter to straighten up any ragged edges of the stacked felt. Then cut the stacked felt into small squares or rectangles.

3 make sewing hole in middle of square

Use a large-eyed sewing needle to make a hole in the center of the square bead.

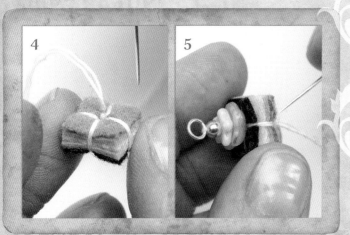

4 stitch through square

Thread a beading needle with embroidery floss and tie a knot in the end. Bring the needle through the hole in the center of the square bead and around one side, then back through the center hole. Repeat for the remaining sides.

5 add beads and jump ring

Thread 1 or more beads and a closed ring onto the thread, and then bring the needle back through the layered felt. Tie off the thread and trim the end. Add the bead to the charm bracelet with a jump ring.

roll-up bead

1 spray felt rectangle with glue

Cut a piece of felt to 4" × 1¼" (10cm × 3cm). Working outside or in a well-ventilated area, spray 1 side of the rectangle with multipurpose spray adhesive.

2 roll up felt rectangle

Roll the rectangle into a long skinny roll. Allow the glue to dry.

3 cut roll

Cut the felt roll into slices.

4 embellish beads

Wrap the beads with ricrac, and sew seed beads around them to embellish.

jelly roll bead

1 cut felt and spray with glue

Cut 2 small pieces of felt in different colors. The bottom piece of felt will be the outside color of the bead, and it should be about ¼" (6mm) wider than the top piece. Working outside or in a well-ventilated area, spray both pieces of felt with multipurpose spray adhesive. Adhere the 2 pieces of felt with the sticky side of the top piece facing up.

2 roll felt pieces together

Starting at the long end of the felt, quickly roll the felt into a tight roll. Hold the roll closed until the adhesive sets. Let the roll dry before slicing.

3 slice roll

After the felt roll has dried, slice off jelly roll beads using sharp scissors or a rotary cutter. Embellish the felt roll with stitching and glass beads.

sushi roll bead

1 spray felt with adhesive

Place strips of scrap felt on the wrong side of a 3" × 4" (8cm × 10cm) felt rectangle, allowing the ends of the scrap strips to hang over the edge. Place your felt rectangle with the strips on a piece of scrap paper outside or in a well-ventilated area. Spray the felt evenly with multipurpose spray adhesive.

2 roll felt up

Starting at one long edge, quickly roll the felt up tightly. Hold the roll closed until the adhesive sets. After the felt roll has dried, slice off sushi roll beads using sharp scissors or a rotary cutter.

vintage glass & wool bead
necklace

My favorite color is the pale blue of my studio walls, so I was thrilled when I found a lovely rosary necklace in a secondhand store that was just the same shade. I removed the broken cross and a few of the beads that were cracked. The little saint is mostly worn off, but I adored it and wanted to use it as a focal point for hanging the glass crystal pendant and little silver bell.

The tiniest-ever velvet millinery flowers from an old hat are glued on the sides of the felt diamond beads, then stitched with embroidery floss and silver seed beads. The wool beads are spaced between wire-wrapped sections of mercury glass garland and glass crystal beads in an unusual pairing that will be a bit fragile—but I love the finished look and have decided if I break one of the beads I will just wire on a new one!

materials

thin, tightly felted wool scraps

6 small millinery flowers

silver seed beads

polyester fiberfill

rosary necklace

4 glass garland beads

16 crystal beads

chandelier crystal

blue bead and silver bell charm

26-gauge silver wire

sewing needle and thread

embroidery floss and needle

tacky glue

freezer paper

round-nose pliers

wire cutters

scissors

iron

pencil

diamond bead

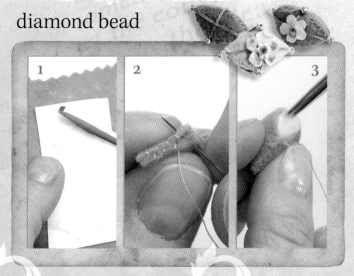

1 cut out diamonds
Trace the patterns on page 126 onto freezer paper and iron them shiny side down onto a small piece of felt. Cut out the 3 felt diamonds.

2 sew diamonds together
Sew the first 2 felt diamonds together along 1 side.

3 stuff and sew bead
Pin the third diamond in place and sew along the second side. Begin sewing the third side, joining the first and third diamonds together. Leave a small opening to add the polyester fiberfill. After the diamond is stuffed, finish sewing the felt shapes together. Tie off the thread and clip the ends.

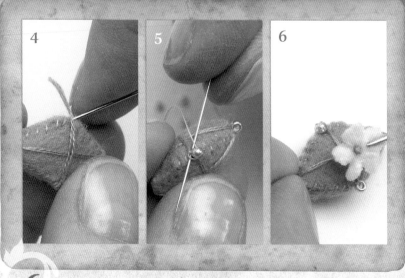

4 stitch crosses onto diamond

Thread an embroidery needle with 2 strands of embroidery floss and stitch a cross over each diamond, sewing from point to point.

5 sew beads onto diamond

Sew a small silver seed bead at each point of the diamond (5 beads total), making sure the 2 end beads are very secure as you will be threading wire through the beads to attach the felt diamond to your jewelry.

6 glue flowers to bead

Glue a ⅜" (1cm) millinery flower in the center of the felt diamond around the bead (3 flowers total). Repeat steps 1 through 6 to make a second diamond bead.

wire-wrapped sections

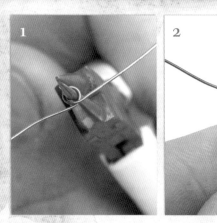

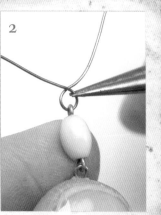

1 make loop in one end of wire

Cut a 6" (15cm) section of 26-gauge wire. Grip the wire with round-nose pliers 2" (5cm) from the end and wrap the wire around the pliers to make a loop.

2 slide beaded segment onto wire

Slide 1 segment of the rosary chain onto the loop.

3 wrap loop

Holding the loop sideways with round-nose pliers, begin wrapping the short wire around the base of the loop several times to make a loose overlapping wire wrap. Clip the wire end, and tuck it in.

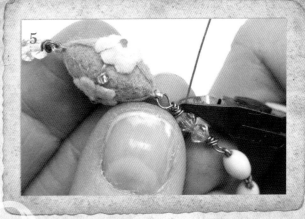

4 *continue linking beaded segments*

Slide on the beads you like and secure the beaded segment to the rosary chain with another wire-wrapped loop. Closely trim the wire end with wire cutters. Continue linking beaded segments to the chain with wire-wrapped loops, always trimming the end of the wire close to the wrap and tucking the end into the wrap. Adjust the angle of the wire loops as needed so the beaded sections hang straight.

5 *link felt diamonds to necklace*

At the point in the necklace where you'd like the felt diamond bead to go, slide the free end of a wire-wrapped segment through the bead at 1 tip of the diamond, make a loop and finish the wire wrap as usual. Slide another section of wire through the bead at the opposite tip of the diamond and wire wrap it in place. Continue linking beaded segments as before.

6 *finish necklace*

Finish the necklace by adding a large central dangle. I wire wrapped a chandelier crystal to a rosary bead and linked it to the saint charm in the center of the necklace. Then I used heavy-gauge wire to create a dangle with a blue bead and a small bell to hang from the bottom of the chandelier crystal.

flower *ball* rings

All my finished felted wool balls are gathered in a pretty bowl on my desk. I had been placing them there one at a time as I finished them, and as the days went by the bowl began to get fuller and fuller. One day a large bead rolled out of the bowl and landed next to a ring blank I had sitting on my desk. This gave me the idea to try to make a series of funky rings with my brightly colored felt balls. I cut the balls in half so they would rest flush against the silver base and began decorating them. They ended up looking a bit like 1950s molded Jell-O salads and noxious insects, but my teenage daughters loved them!

materials

ring blank

⅞" (2cm) felted wool ball

wool felt scraps

circle template

selection of beads
and sew-on gems

small scraps of ricrac

sewing needle

thread

tacky glue

E6000 adhesive

scallop-edge scissors

scissors

1 make felt ball and measure

See pages 16–17 for complete instructions on making a wet-felted ball. Start with a bigger ball than the size of bead you want, then continue felting your bead to the hard-bead stage. Use a circle template to gauge the size of your bead.

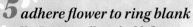

2 cut felted bead in half

Cut the felted bead in half with a pair of sharp scissors.

3 cut out circle base

Select the circle the next size up from your bead to trace the background for the flower ball. Cut around the circle using a pair of scallop-edge scissors. Line up the point of the scallop with the edge of the circle.

more ideas...

Adorn your rings with bits of narrow ricrac, tiny flowers and decorative stitching.

4 embellish half bead

Glue the half bead on the right side of the scallop circle using tacky glue. Let it dry. With a needle and thread, sew beads, gems or felt circles over the wool felt bead. Tie off the thread and clip the ends.

5 adhere flower to ring blank

Use E6000 to adhere the felt flower to a ring blank, and let it dry.

skeleton
bracelet

It was Halloween and we were making polymer clay figures at my art group to use in spooky shadow boxes. When I brought my skeleton man home I couldn't bear to glue him in a box, so I designed a bracelet around him so I could wear him everywhere. My favorite element in this bracelet is the wool and paper beads. My daughter Marina was in my studio the day I was putting the skeleton bracelet together. She was playing around with some book paper pages, rolling them into beads and layering them with gel medium to make a thick stack. We started experimenting with the paper shapes and sewed some onto the wool beads for a very funky look. The elastic bead cord attached easily to the skeleton's wire hands with crimp beads. The rest of the wool beads and found objects are threaded on the stretchy cord for a fun, creepy bracelet.

materials

- black wool roving
- wool felt scraps
- several red glass flower beads
- black polymer clay
- white polymer clay
- 28-gauge wire
- coated wire
- 2 black E beads
- pages from an old book
- sewing needle and thread

- assorted beads and found objects, including a vintage clothing tag (optional)
- white and red embroidery floss and needle
- 8mm clear elastic bead cord (Beadalon)
- 2 crimp beads
- jump rings
- eyelet

- tacky glue
- gel medium
- wire cutters
- round-nose pliers
- crimping pliers
- Japanese screw punch
- eyelet setter and small hammer
- scissors
- self-healing cutting mat

flower bun bead

1 wrap felted bead with embroidery floss

Make 2 soft-felted wool beads with black wool roving. Also make 4 hard-felted black wool beads and set them aside. See pages 16–17 for instructions on making wet-felted beads. Allow all the wool beads to completely dry. With 2 strands of white embroidery floss and an embroidery needle, stitch up through the center of a soft-felted bead. Wrap the floss around the bead and poke the needle up through the same spot in the center. Pull the floss snug. Wrap the floss around the bead again on the other side, and poke the needle through the same center spot. Pull the floss snug. Repeat until there is a total of 5 wraps.

2 sew flower bead on top of wool bead

After the last wrap, pull the needle up through the center of the bead and thread on a glass flower bead. Make a French knot on the top of the glass bead by wrapping the floss around the needle 4 times and poking it back through the glass flower and the felt bead. See page 19 for instructions on making a French knot. Pull the floss snug against the needle as you pull it through the felt bead. Stitch a second glass flower bead onto the back of the wool bead using a French knot to hold it in place. Tie off the floss and clip the ends. Repeat to create a second flower bun bead.

TIP

A very soft felt bead will have a lot of fluff around the floss wraps, and a firmer felt bead will have less puffing around the floss.

paper-stitched bead

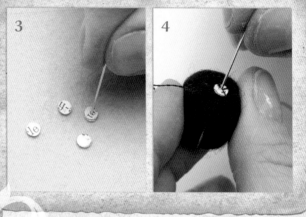

1 make wool beads and word circles
Glue together 2 pages of text with gel medium, and let the stacked pages dry.

2 punch word circles
Use a Japanese screw punch to make several word circles from the layered paper.

3 make holes in word circles
Use a sharp needle to make a hole in the center of each word circle.

4 sew word circles onto bead
Use red embroidery floss and a sewing needle to stitch the word circles to 1 of the hard-felted black wool beads (from step 1 on page 91).

fabric charm

1 punch hole in tag shape
Cut out a small felt tag shape. Place the felt piece on a cutting mat and punch a hole in 1 side with a Japanese screw punch.

2 set eyelet
Insert an eyelet into the hole you punched. Hit it lightly with a small hammer to set the eyelet in the felt.

3 embellish felt charm
Sew on a bit of ephemera for decoration. I used a vintage tag torn from an old child's coat.

4 add beads to charm
Wire wrap 2 beads together and link them to the charm with a jump ring.

finished bracelet

2 flatten crimp bead

Secure the strung bracelet by flattening the crimp bead with crimping pliers.

1 string bracelet

Make a skeleton out of white and black polymer clay. Insert short pieces of coated wire into his body for legs, and link the head and body with a short piece of wire as well. Make a loop in 1 end of 2 more short wire pieces with round-nose pliers. Stick the straight ends into the body to make arms. Press 2 E beads into the face for eyes, and draw lines for a mouth. Bake the skeleton at 275° F for 15 minutes (or follow manufacturer's specifications). Allow him to cool. Cut 10" (25cm) of 8mm clear elastic bead cord and thread on a combination of wool beads, glass beads and charms. When you've finished beading, run the needle through a crimp bead, through the skeleton's arm, and then back through the crimp bead.

3 finish bracelet

Turn the flattened crimp bead on its side and move it to the groove nearest the tip of the crimping pliers. Use the pliers to fold the crimp bead in half, and trim the elastic cord. Secure the remaining free end of the elastic cord in the same manner, pulling the cord tight until the bracelet fits comfortably before crimping it in place and trimming the end.

If you like, embellish the skeleton. Stitch a vintage label onto a felt rectangle, then stitch around the skeleton's neck, arms and legs to secure the background.

another idea...

Changing the color scheme creates a bracelet with a completely different look. Stitch blue beads with a cross of red embroidery floss, and then add a tiny green glass flower in the center. String a combination of felt flower buns and glass beads on a length of elastic cord to make a bright bracelet.

lotus *flower*
ring

I first made the lotus ring in a metal clay ring class taught by Sherri Haab. Instead of using stones or sculpted clay, I wanted to try to create a wool felt focal point for my ring. I created a sewn felt flower with the petals dipped in silver glass glitter to get the look I wanted. The fine glass glitter adds an elegant finish to the pale felt, along with the wired glass bead stamens and vintage button center. A simpler version of this ring can be made by gluing or sewing the felt flower to a premade ring base. This ring makes such a pretty gift.

materials

scraps of pale pink wool felt

ring blank

fine glass glitter

approximately 12" (30cm)
    of 30-gauge silver wire

5 silver-lined clear seed beads

vintage rhinestone button

E6000

tacky glue

sewing needle and thread

paintbrush

scissors

wire cutters

Template for the petals shown at actual size.

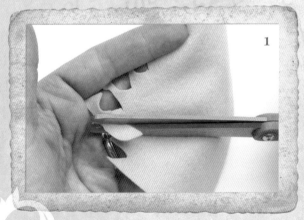

1 cut out petals
Cut out 8 petals freehand from a square of felt. If you'd rather work from a pattern, you may use the template provided on this page instead.

2 apply glue to petal edges
Mix a bit of water with some tacky glue until the mixture reaches the consistency of cream. Dip your finger or a paintbrush into the mixture and spread it along the cut edges of a petal.

3 glitter edges of petals
Dip the felt petal in fine glass glitter and shake off the excess. Repeat for the remaining 7 petals. Set the petals aside to dry.

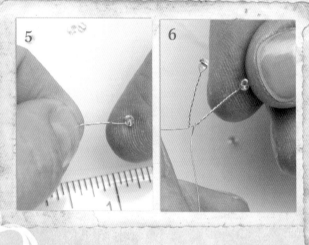

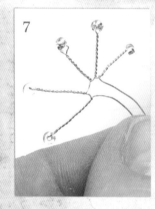

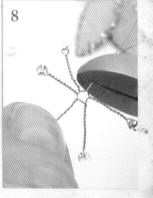

4 *sew petals together*

Arrange your petals into 2 layers, creating an inner and an outer layer. Thread a needle with matching thread, and begin sewing the first 2 inside petals, tacking them together with thread and overlapping the petal bases slightly. Add the other 2 center petals, tacking each 1 in place by sewing through the base each time. Begin sewing the 4 outside petals in place by spacing them in between the 4 center petals and tacking them in place. Set the flower aside.

5 *make stamens*

To make the wired bead stamens, begin with 12" (30cm) of 30-gauge silver wire. String on 1 silver-lined clear seed bead. Bend the wire end over at 1½" (4cm) with the seed bead in the wire fold. Begin twisting the bead between the right thumb and fore-finger while holding the 2 wire ends in the left hand ½" (1cm) away from the bead. Continue twisting the bead until the wire twist is in a ½" (1cm) long even twist right up to the bottom of the bead.

6 *continue to twist stamens*

Thread another seed bead onto the long wire end, and make another fold ½" (1cm) away from the wire twist. Twist the bead until the wire is in a nice even twist next to the first twist.

7 *continue making stamens*

Continue adding beads and twisting the wire until you have 5 glass beads on twisted wire stamens.

8 *finish stamens*

Twist the 2 wire ends together and clip off the excess wire.

9 sew stamens to flower center

Arrange the stamens evenly in a circle, and use a sewing needle and thread to sew the beaded stamens in the center of the lotus flower.

10 sew on rhinestone center

Sew a rhinestone button in the center of the flower over the wired stamens. Tie off the thread and clip the ends.

11 adhere flower to ring base

Shape the beaded wire stamens to curve around the rhinestone button. Use E6000 to adhere the lotus flower to a ring base, and let it dry.

more ideas...

If you'd like, you can make ring bases out of metal clay, as shown here. When you create the base, make a small silver cup for the felt flower to rest in. Drill two small holes in the ring before firing so the felt flowers can be sewn in place using Nymo nylon beading thread.

playthings

GATHERED IN THIS CHAPTER YOU WILL FIND FANCIFUL PROJECTS TO INSPIRE YOUR CREATIVITY AND PUT YOU IN A PLAYFUL MOOD. Whimsical fairies (see page 108), angels (see page 112) and tiny *Stuffed Chicks* (see page 104) made of bits of wool and felt delight the young at heart. A traveling art satchel filled with colored pencils and a notepad makes a charming gift for a young artist and has two handy handles for easy transport (see page 116). Or wrap your brushes in a soft roll of felt to travel to your next art retreat (see page 120).

Whether you prefer to make something functional to aid in your creative play, such as a pincushion scented with dried lavender (see page 100), or something purely frivolous, this chapter has the perfect little plaything for you.

pincushion
pillow

Wool felt is the perfect fabric to use for a pincushion, as it provides a sturdy base for your pins and needles. Fragrant dried lavender is stuffed inside a cushion of wool roving so the pincushion releases a wonderful fragrance each time you use it. The off-center flower design is a fun use for your favorite tiny felt scraps and any unusual vintage things you may have collected.

materials

*scraps of wool felt
   in coordinating colors*

assorted cotton print fabric

glass beads

embroidery floss and needle

dried lavender

polyester fiberfill or wool roving

freezer paper

circle template

scallop-edge scissors

straight pins

sewing needle and thread

scissors

sewing machine and thread

iron

pincushion

1 sew around square and trim corners

Cut 1 4½" × 4½" (11cm × 11cm) square of wool and 1 4½" × 4½" (11cm × 11cm) square of coordinating cotton print fabric. Pin the squares with right sides together and stitch around the edges with a ¼" (6mm) seam allowance, leaving a 2" (5cm) opening for stuffing. Trim the corners of the sewn square, trimming the piece of fabric a bit closer to the stitching line than the felt.

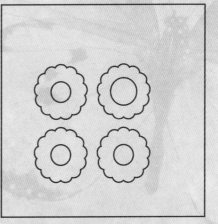

Enlarge the pincushion template to 175% to bring to full size.

2 stuff pincushion

Turn the pincushion right-side out and fill it with dried lavender and wool roving or polyester fiberfill.

3 stitch opening closed

Stitch the opening closed with a sewing needle and thread.

4 cut out flowers and arrange

Use a circle template to trace 4 $\frac{15}{16}$" (2cm) circles on the wrong side of 4 scraps of coordinating felt. Use scallop-edge scissors to cut around the circles for the 4 flowers. Trace 3 $\frac{7}{16}$" (1cm) circles on the dull side of the freezer paper. Roughly cut the circles apart, and iron them shiny-side down to the right side of the felt. Cut out the 3 flower centers. Pin 4 felt flowers in place on the pincushion, referring to the template on page 101 for placement. Tack the center of each flower to the pincushion for placement.

yo yo flower

1 sew around edge of circle

Cut a 1½" (4cm) circle out of cotton print fabric. Turn the outside edge in ¼" (6mm) and finger press around the circle. Sew around the finger-pressed edge with a needle and thread, working in a loose running stitch.

2 gather circle

After stitching all around the circle, pull the thread to gather the circle of fabric, and tie off the thread.

3 sew yo yo onto flower

Stitch the yo yo circle to one of the flowers with a sewing needle and thread.

4

4 embroider flowers

Embroider each of the 4 flowers with stitching. Sew beads to the center of the first flower. Work a running stitch around the yo yo flower center. Work a blanket stitch around the center of another flower, and stitch outward from the center on the same flower. With a needle and embroidery floss, work a daisy over the center of the last flower. (See pages 18–19 for instructions on working in running, blanket and daisy stitches.)

more ideas...

Here are two more ideas for transforming your wool scraps into lovely pincushions.

{1} Sew overlapping pieces of felt and corduroy directly to a vintage red tomato pincushion to make this vintage-inspired variation. Wrap floss tightly around the pincushion to define each section. Add a green felt stem to the pumpkin top with tiny tendrils of florist tape and wire secured beneath.

{2} To make this square version of the pincushion, stitch each circle in place with a blanket stitch for a graphic look.

1

2

stuffed chicks

I recently helped Grandma clean out her attic and found a box of fabric scraps from old curtains, cushions, doll dresses and pieces left over from sewing projects. Inspired by the drawings my children have made over the years, I set out to use some of the small scraps of vintage fabrics to make the creatures of their imaginings. We named these little stuffies "the ickles." They are so tiny they can travel in your pocket to art class or school. It is always a surprise to add the faces at the end and discover each stuffed creature's personality. As each one is named, I embroider their names on their backs. My daughter Olivia says it will be good to have her kitty Mim home again after her adventures getting her picture taken for the book!

materials

cotton fabrics

wool felt scraps

round black beads

embroidery floss and needle

polyester fiberfill

*little ribbons or bells
        for decoration (optional)*

sewing needle and thread

scissors

sewing machine and thread

Templates for the chicks shown at actual size. Choose from three different beak choices and two different wing styles.

1 cut out body pieces

Cut 2 bodies and 4 wings from cotton fabric as well as 2 eyes, a beak and 2 feet from small pieces of felt in different colors. Choose any of the templates on page 105.

2 sew, stuff and pin wings in place

Pin the wing pieces with right sides together, and sew around the stitching lines using a stitch length setting of 2 on your sewing machine. Trim around the stitching if necessary. Turn the wings right side out and stuff them with fiberfill. Pin the wings in place, sandwiched between the 2 body pieces with right sides together.

3 sew around body

Sew around the body, leaving an opening at the bottom of the chick, as indicated on the pattern. Clip around the curved edges so the seam won't pucker.

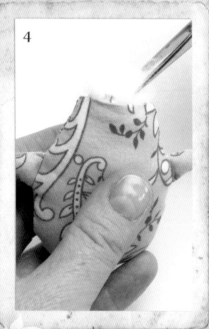

4 stuff chick

Turn the body right side out and fill the chick with fiberfill stuffing. Sew the opening closed with a needle and thread.

5 sew on eyes, beak and feet

Sew the eyes, beak and feet in place by hand using 1 strand of embroidery floss and blanket stitch (shown on page 19.)

6 sew on beads

Sew tiny black beads on the eyes. Add a tiny ribbon bow (or bell) if you like.

more ideas...

Design your own little stuffies. Start with a simple outline, using cotton fabric for the body. Cut features from felt for the faces, and embroider the details.

TIP

Trace patterns using tracing paper and pin them to your fabric. For very detailed shapes, sew right through the tracing paper, following the stitching line. After sewing, tear away the paper and trim the fabric close to the stitching line.

{1} Hooty the owl has big eyes and a funky Amy Butler cotton fabric body. See page 126 for the template.

{2} Mim the cat was drawn by Olivia (age five) just after our cat had kittens. See page 126 for the template.

1

2

TIP

Embroider a tiny name on the back of your little creations. This little stuffie's name is Hooty.

mim

ByOLIVIA

vintage wool-wrapped fairies

I adore the vintage cotton-and-wool ornaments that were made in Germany in the early 1900s. This fairy was an experiment to see if I could recreate one. The real cotton pipe cleaners grab onto the fibers as you twist them around, so you don't need any glue or spray to hold the wool in place. A crinkly-looking wool fiber is easier to use for the body than a fine, smooth roving that slips as you wrap. The fun part is decorating the little crêpe-paper-and-hankie dresses for the fairies. I like adding the tiniest paper chains, star wands for wishing and little decorated felt balls.

materials

2 6″ (15cm) cotton pipe cleaners

combed wool roving

copy of vintage photograph of a child's
    face, cut into a ¾″ (2cm) oval
    (see template on page 126)

book paper

patterned paper
    (for bodice and paper chain)

crêpe paper

floral wire

paper stars

tinsel

mica flakes

fine glass glitter

bits of fabric, felt, lace, tinsel,
    pompoms, buttons, ribbon
    and string to decorate

tacky glue

scallop-edge scissors

scissors

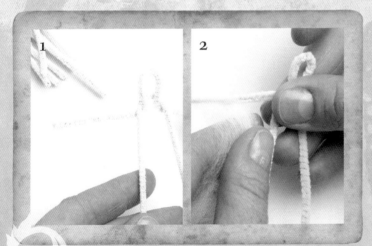

1 twist pipe cleaners to form body base
Bend 2 pipe cleaners into U shapes, and twist them together to make a body shape. Bend both ends of one pipe cleaner up to make arms.

2 wrap leg with roving
Pull out a small piece of roving and begin twisting it around 1 of the pipe cleaner legs. Let the cotton pipe cleaner "grab" the wool fibers as you wrap them around. Start at the foot and wind your way up to the body. Wrap the other leg and both arms, ending each wrap at the waist.

3 wrap head with roving

With a larger piece of wool, begin wrapping the head, and end the wrap around the waist. Wrap a little more wool around the body if it needs a bit of plumping up.

Bend the arms to shape them and make 2 feet by bending up the ends of the legs.

4 make skirt and attach

Cut a piece of crêpe paper to 1½" × 6" (4cm × 15cm). Scallop one edge with scissors, and add a dusting of mica on the skirt if desired. Begin gathering the skirt around the body using tacky glue to attach it to the fairy.

5 make bodice and attach

Glue little sleeve straps over the shoulders. Use the template on page 126 to make a bodice of cut patterned paper, felt or fabric. Glue the bodice to the doll's chest. Wrap a ribbon around the waist and tie it in back.

8 make hat

Copy the hat template on page 126, and cut out a hat from decorative paper or book paper and roll it into a cone shape. Glue the straight edges together with tacky glue. Decorate the hat with glitter, tinsel or paper stars.

6 embellish clothes

Glue a bit of tinsel in the middle of the ribbon, and glue a button in the center of the bodice.

7 adhere face to doll

Glue the face to the wool head.

9 *finish hat*

Glue a tinsel pompom on the point of the hat, then glue it onto the fairy's head.

10 *create wand*

Glue 2 stars back to back, sandwiching a 1½" (4cm) piece of floral wire between them. Cover the stars with glue and dip them in fine glass glitter. Glue the wand in one of the fairy's hands and prop it in place until the glue dries.

11 *create paper chain*

Cut out and glue together a tiny paper chain, and tie it with string to the fairy's other hand.

another idea...

The Halloween fairy is holding a little pumpkin made from a felt ball decorated with embroidery floss and felt scraps. She has a little black washer on her hat and a dress made with crêpe paper, wool felt and a piece of a sheer black hankie.

glitter

angels

It is so fun to find the delicate ornaments made in Japan in the 1950s. I purchased a little bag of very smashed angel ornaments that had glue melted through the thin dresses, leaving terrible brown stains. The bodies were made of cardboard with spun cotton heads. The shape was so similar to the wood figure bases at my craft store that I decided to try to remake the little angels. The heads are painted with acrylic paint and the bases are wrapped with felt. An old wedding veil with a lovely edge was used for the overskirt with some German paper scrap wings glued to the back. The figure base is basic enough that the clothing could be easily adapted to make a princess, a fairy or a witch!

materials

2" (5cm) wood base (Lara's Crafts)

light pink and light blue scraps
    of wool felt

tulle

chenille stems or wired tinsel

tiny greenery, candle or tree bulb

silver paper wings

fine glass glitter

mica flakes

black, red, white and flesh-tone acrylic
    paint (Delta Ceramcoat)

tacky glue

black Micron pen (Pigma 005)

Quickie glue pen (Sakura)

paintbrushes

sewing needle and thread

scissors

pencil

Template for the angel faces and skirt shown at actual size.

1 paint doll's head

Paint the head and neck of the wood base with flesh-colored acrylic paint. Allow the paint to dry. Pencil in the eyes and mouth using the template on page 113. Draw the outline for the eyes with a black micron pen.

2 paint on mouth and eyes

With a small paintbrush and some red paint, outline the mouth. With black paint, fill in the eyes. Add a tiny dot of white paint to each eye when the black paint is dry.

3 apply glue to hairline

After the paint is dry, sketch on the hairline with a pencil. Trace over the pencil line with a glue pen.

4 apply glitter to hairline

Dust the glue line with fine glass glitter.

5 apply glitter to hair

Spread tacky glue onto the doll's head for her hair, and cover it with glass glitter. Use a soft, dry paintbrush to brush away excess glitter.

6 create dress and attach to doll

Cut out the wool dress using the pattern on page 113. Cover the wood base with tacky glue and fold the wool dress around the base.

7 gather tulle

With a needle and thread, sew a running stitch along the top edge of a 2" × 9" (5cm × 23cm) piece of tulle. Pull the thread to gather the tulle.

8 sew on tulle

Wrap the gathered tulle around the doll. Tack the tulle to the back of the wool dress with a needle and thread.

9 create arms

Cut a 2¾" (7cm) piece of wired tinsel or chenille stem and bend it into an arm shape. Bend 1 hand around a piece of greenery or a tiny candle or tree bulb. Glue the arms onto the figure with tacky glue.

10 glitter halo

Cut a ⅞" (2cm) felt circle. Spread a thin layer of tacky glue over the surface of the circle and cover it with mica flakes. Shake off the excess mica, and glue the halo to the back of the angel.

11 adhere wings to angel

Attach the silver wings to the back of the figure with tacky glue.

mini *art* satchel

Tucked inside this traveling art satchel is everything a little artist needs while on the go. The felt pockets inside are a perfect fit for colored pencils and a small notebook. The felt handles are sized just right for tiny hands. Cut thin strips of felt to spell the name of your little artist and stitch the letters to the cover of the satchel. You may want to tuck a small pair of scissors or a few pages of stickers inside. Art to go...

materials

felt in multiple colors

embroidery floss and needle

composition notebook, 3½" × 4½" (9cm × 11cm)

small colored pencils, 3½" (9cm) long

small millinery flowers or circles of felt

water-soluble marker

straight pins

sewing machine and thread

tacky glue

scissors

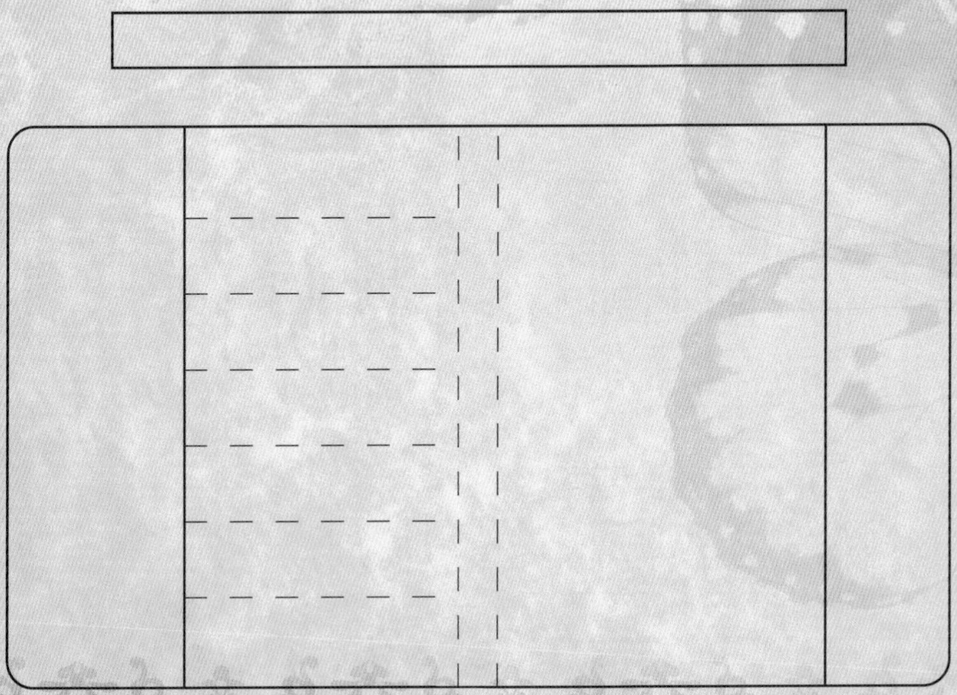

Enlarge the pattern for the mini art satchel by 175% to bring to full size.

1 cut and mark felt pieces

Cut 1 9¼" × 5¾" (24cm × 15cm) rectangle of blue felt and round off the corners. Cut 1 5¾" x 6⅜" (15cm × 16cm) rectangle of purple felt. Mark sewing lines on the felt using a water-soluble marker and the pattern on page 117.

2 sew along marked lines

Pin the felt pieces together with the center line on the pattern marking the placement of the purple felt. Test to see if the notebook and pencils fit. Adjust the seam lines as necessary. Use a sewing machine to sew along the marked stitching lines, beginning with the edges and leaving a ⅛" (3mm) seam allowance. Backstitch at the beginning and end of each line of stitching. (See page 18 for instructions on working in backstitch.) Trim the threads.

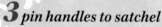

3 pin handles to satchel

Cut 4 6¾" × ½" (17cm × 1cm) rectangles of yellow-green felt for the handles. Measure in 1" (3cm) from the sides of the satchel and mark the handle placement. Pin the felt strips together with 1 on each side to make sturdy handles. Machine-sew or hand-stitch the handles in place at each end of the art satchel.

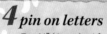

4 pin on letters

Cut ¼" (6mm) wide strips of felt in different colors for the monogram letters. Arrange them on the front of the art satchel to spell out the little artist's name. Pin the letters in place.

5 sew letters in place

Sew the letters in place using 2 strands of embroidery floss. Glue on little flowers or circles of felt to dot the i's.

6 fill satchel

Insert colored pencils and a small notebook inside the satchel for the little artist to use.

paintbrush
roll

I wanted to give my friend Candice a lovely set of new paint-brushes for her birthday. One day when I was shopping at my art store, I found several assorted sets of brushes with amazingly smooth white handles. I gathered them up in my basket, and home I went to design a pretty pouch for them. I was sitting at my desk when I spied a lovely piece of taupe felt in the suitcase of wool pieces I keep by my sewing machine. It was just the right size to fold over the handles, and it was wide enough to allow me to line up the brushes side by side. The brushes can be rolled up for traveling so they'll be protected by the felt. I was so excited to give my friend the beautiful brushes all rolled up and tied with a chocolate brown velvet ribbon. I think of it as an artful reminder that simple things do matter.

materials

large piece of felt

ribbon seam binding

24" (61cm) of velvet ribbon

vintage silk flower

water-soluble pen

straight pins

scallop-edge scissors

ruler

paintbrushes

sewing machine and thread

sewing needle and thread

iron

scissors

1 iron seam binding

Cut a piece of felt into a 14¼" × 14¼" (36cm × 36cm) square. Fold 1 side of the square up to make a 4¾" (12cm) pocket. Iron the folded felt. Cut approximately 16" (41cm) of ribbon seam binding and fold it in half. Iron the folded seam binding to set the crease.

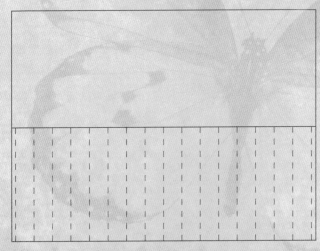

Enlarge the template for the paintbrush roll by 400% to bring to full size.

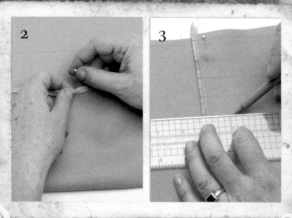

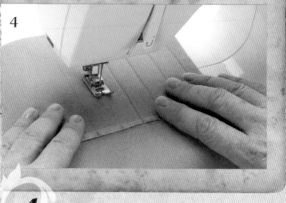

2 pin seam binding along pocket edge

Slide the folded seam binding onto the pocket edge of the felt square so that half of the seam binding covers either side of the pocket's edge. Pin the seam binding in place. Sew the seam binding to the pocket edge using a sewing machine.

4 sew along marked lines

Sew along each line you marked for the paintbrush pockets using a sewing machine.

3 mark seam lines inside roll

With a water-soluble pen, draw lines just inside the top and side edges of the paintbrush roll to mark where you'll cut the scalloped edge. Then lay the first paintbrush to be included in the roll in the pocket. Place a pin on either side of the paintbrush and draw a line where each pin is placed. Continue to pin paintbrushes in place and draw lines until each paintbrush is accounted for. This way you'll have pockets sized specifically for each brush.

5 cut scalloped edges

Cut along the top and side edges of the roll with scallop-edge scissors.

6 sew ribbon to roll

Cut each end of a 24" (61cm) length of velvet ribbon on the diagonal with scallop-edge scissors. Fold the ribbon approximately in half and pin the ribbon at this halfway point to the brush roll just above the pocket on the left side. Sew the ribbon to the felt, stitching a square small enough so it will be covered up by the flower.

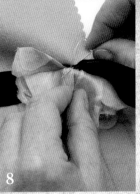

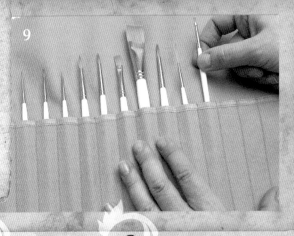

7 take apart silk flower

Remove a vintage silk flower from an old hat or any other source by snipping the threads securing the flower. If the flower is glued on, you may want to remove the bottom layer of petals because the glue may not come off. Also, if the flower is larger than you'd like, you may remove petals until the flower is the size that works for your project.

8 sew on flower

Use a sewing needle and thread to attach the flower to the brush roll on top of the square where the ribbon is sewn.

9 insert brushes into roll

Slide all the brushes into their customized pockets, roll up your brush roll and tie it with the velvet ribbon.

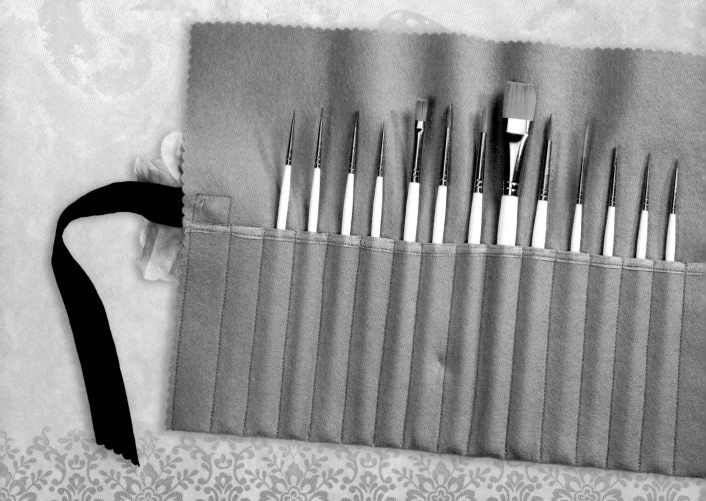

resources

Most of the supplies you'll need can be found at local craft stores and discount department stores. It's also fun to incorporate vintage finds into your work. If you're having trouble finding what you need locally, use this list of resources to locate supplies and tools. Almost every business has a Web site these days, so make sure to search online.

Wool Felt

Blackberry Primitives
(402) 423-8464
www.blackberryprimitives.com
hand-dyed wool, wool fabric

Magic Cabin
(888) 623-3655
www.magiccabin.com
wool felt

Mary Flanagan Woolens
(920) 589-2221
www.mfwoolens.com
hand-dyed wool, wool fabric

Ornamentea/Bedizen Ornaments
(919) 834-6260
www.ornamentea.com
wool roving, wool beads, felt, needle-felting materials, jewelry findings, glass glitter

Weeks Dye Works
(919) 772-9166
www.weeksdyeworks.com
over-dyed embroidery threads, over-dyed wool

The Wool Den
(513) 933-0102
www.wool-den.com
hand-dyed and solid wool felt

Sewing Supplies

Carma
www.carma.biz
hand-dyed ribbons, trims, velvet, fibers, ricrac, seam binding

Clover Needlecraft, Inc.
(800) 233-1703
www.clover-usa.com
needle-felting tools, appliqué pins, sewing notions

Corn Wagon Quilt Co.
(801) 491-3551
www.cornwagonquilts.com
hand-dyed wools, embroidery threads, sewing notions, quilting fabrics

The DMC Corporation
(973) 589-0606
www.dmc-usa.com
cotton pearl thread, embroidery floss

Piecemakers Country Store
(714) 641-3112
www.piecemakers.com
fine sewing and appliqué needles

Vintage Items

Abe Books
www.abebooks.com
vintage books

Alibris
www.alibris.com
vintage books

Castle in the Air
(510) 204-9801
ribbons, millinery flowers, crêpe paper, German scrap, unusual papers

Cat's Cradle
(801) 374-1832
www.catscradlegallery.com
objects of interest and antiquity, vintage ribbon and trim, vintage millinery, paper lace, vintage jewelry

D. Blumchen and Company
(866) 653-9627
www.blumchen.com
vintage millinery, stamens, Dresden paper flowers and wings, Lametta tinsel trims, bullion crinkle wire, diamond dust glass glitter, crêpe paper, paper lace, cotton chenille stems, candle clips

Dolls and Lace
(801) 836-8769
www.dollsandlace.com
vintage millinery flowers, stamens, trim, vintage ribbons, paper lace, vintage fabric, vintage photos and ephemera

Lacis Museum of Lace and Textiles
(510) 843-7290
www.lacis.com
stamens, millinery supplies, vintage lace and ribbons

Manto Fev
(402) 505-3752
www.mantofev.com
tiny bells, vintage lace and trims, vintage jewelry, paper ephemera

Victorian Scrap Works
(717) 314-2250
www.victorianscrapworks.com
German scrap, Dresden flowers and wings, silver crinkle wire bullion, silver Lametta tinsel wire

Wild Hair Studio
(253) 770-0544
www.wildhairstudio.com
vintage beads and sequins, sew-on gems

Jewelry Supplies

Artbeads
(253) 857-3433
www.artbeads.com
sterling silver wire and jump rings, jewelry tools and findings, beads

Beadcats
(503) 625-2323
www.beadcats.com
glass flower beads, seed beads, beading supplies

Kit Kraft
(818) 509-9739
www.kitkraft.biz
ring blanks, vintage sequins

Sherri Haab
www.sherrihaab.com
ring blanks, jewelry findings

General Supplies

Avery Dennison
(800) 462-8379
www.avery.com
permanent glue stick

Burnt Offerings Studio
(440) 259-2271
www.burntofferings.com
tin shears

Creative Impressions
(719) 596-4860
www.creativeimpressions.com
acrylic gridded metal-edged ruler

Duncan Enterprises
(800) 438-6226
www.duncancrafts.com
Aleene's tacky glue

Eclectic Products, inc.
(800) 767-4667
www.E-6000.com
E-6000 clear industrial-strength adhesive

EK Success
www.eksuccess.com
flower punch

Elmer's
www.elmers.com
craft bond spray adhesive

Fiskars Brands, Inc.
(866) 348-5661
www.fiskars.com
scallop-edge scissors, pinking shears, rotary cutter, self-healing mat, fine-point scissors

Golden Artist Colors, Inc.
(607) 847-6154
www.goldenpaints.com
acrylic paint, fluid acrylics, gel medium

Lara's Crafts
(800) 232-5272
www.larascrafts.com
wood figure bases, girl game piece

Rags-n-Tags
www.rags-n-tags.com
glass glitter, mica flakes

Rose Art Industries, Inc.
(800) 272-9667
www.megabrands.com
mini colored pencils

Sakura of America
www.sakuraofamerica.com
Quickie Glue pen, Micron pens

Sanford Corporation
(800) 323-0749
www.sharpie.com
Sharpie markers

Staedtler Incorporated
(800) 776-5544
www.staedtler.com
circle template

Traditions Year-Round Holiday Store
(800) 538-2446
www.christmastraditions.com
glass bead garland, tinsel

Volcano Arts
www.volcanoarts.biz
Japanese screw punch, crimp beads and crimp bead pliers, eyelets and eyelet-setting tools

X-Acto
www.xacto.com
X-Acto knife and refill blades

Dyes

Dharma Trading Co.
(800) 542-5227
www.dharmatrading.com
fabric dyes

Making Memories
(801) 294-0430
www.makingmemories.com
scrapbook dyes

Ranger Industries, Inc.
(732) 389-3535
www.rangerink.com
Distress Ink dye

W. Cushing & Company
(800) 626-7847
www.wcushing.com
dyes

Thrift Stores

Deseret Industries
www.deseretindustries.com

Goodwill Industries
www.goodwill.org

The Salvation Army
www.satruck.com

Savers
(425) 462-1515
www.savers.com

Online Auction

eBay
www.ebay.com
needle books, vintage crêpe paper, vintage buttons and jewelry pieces, rosary necklaces, glass garlands, metal zippers, seam binding and anything your little heart desires that you can't find anywhere else

templates

contributing

artists

Susan Edmonson
www.susanedmonsondesigns.com
Treasure Box, page 41

Candice Elton
www.thesparrowspost.blogspot.com
Christmas Tree variation, page 37

Sherri Haab
www.sherrihaab.com
charms in Felt Charm Bracelet, page 76

Adrienne Keith
charms in Felt Charm Bracelet, page 76

Wendy Wallin-Mallinow
charms in Felt Charm Bracelet, page 76

Kristin Steiner
www.kristinsteiner.com
Treasure Box, page 41

Enlarge the templates for Hooty the owl (see page 107) by 150% to bring to actual size.

Enlarge the template for Mim the cat (see page 107) by 150% to bring to actual size.

Enlarge the template for the cone bead (see page 77) by 150% to bring to actual size.

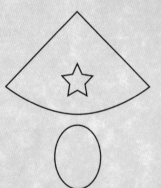

Enlarge the templates for the fairy hat (top), face (middle) and bodice (bottom) (see page 109) by 150% to bring to actual size.

Enlarge the template for the diamond bead (see page 85) by 150% to bring to actual size.

find more crafty inspiration in these North Light titles...

Sweet Needle Felts

by Jenn Docherty

Sweet Needle Felts features all the techniques and information you will need to begin needle felting, including step-by-step instructions for 25 adorable projects. Learn how to create wearable items such as jewelry, scarves, hats and bags. Decorate your home with cozy pillows and rugs. Needle felt huggable, loveable dolls and toys, including author Jenn Docherty's signature bear. Using just a few simple tools, turn soft, warm wool into colorful creations to wear, give and hug!

ISBN-10: 1-60061-039-0, ISBN-13: 978-1-60061-039-4, paperback, 128 pages, Z1490

Warm Fuzzies

by Betz White

Warm Fuzzies is filled with techniques, tips and patterns for creating 30 cute and colorful felted projects, including cozy pillows and throws as well as comfortable hats, scarves, pincushions and handbags. Author Betz White will show you how to felt thrift store and bargain sweaters, then cut them up and use them to make quick, adorable projects for the whole family. Learn how to select the best knitted wool for felting, the best way to full it, and how to combine this process with a wide variety of other techniques, including appliqué, knitted I-cord, basic embroidery, needle felting, pre-felting manipulation and more.

ISBN-10: 1-60061-007-2, ISBN-13: 978-1-60061-007-3, paperback, 144 pages, Z1026

Simply Beaded Bliss

by Heidi Boyd

If you love beading but would also like to try incorporating some handmade elements into your jewelry projects, this is just the book for you. Choose from more than 40 beaded projects, including jewelry, gifts and cards, featuring dynamic mixed-media elements made from diverse materials such as polymer clay, scrapbook embellishments, wire, sequins, buttons, and even nuts and bolts. Each project embodies Heidi Boyd's pretty and simple style.

ISBN-10: 1-60061-095-1, ISBN-13: 978-1-60061-095-0, paperback, 144 pages, Z2004

Pretty Little Things

by Sally Jean Alexander

Learn how to use vintage ephemera, found objects, old photographs and scavenged text to make playful, pretty little things, including charms, vials, miniature shrines, reliquary boxes and much more. Sally Jean's easy and accessible soldering techniques for capturing collages within glass make for whimsical projects, and her all-around magical style makes this charming book a crafter's fairytale.

ISBN-10: 1-58180-842-9 , ISBN-13: 978-1-58180-842-1, paperback, 128 pages, Z0012

These and other fine North Light Books are available at your local craft retailer, bookstore or online supplier. Or visit our web site at www.mycraftivity.com.